PUBLISHING
& associates

Endorsements

"Tim Herzog offers an insightful perspective on the generational challenges impacting societal norms and culture. The Foundation We Stand Upon highlights the relationship between faith, society, and the ever-changing family structure." –Johnny Weiss, MSW, University of Cincinnati.

"Tim does a great job explaining, through multiple examples of scripture, scientific comparisons, and common sense, that God truly and clearly exists and has a plan. This book is written in an understandable style; not just for the theologian but for any layperson from all walks of life as well." –Brian Mallette, Bachelor of Science in Youth Ministry, Cincinnati Christian University."

The Foundation We Stand Upon

TIM HERZOG

bush
PUBLISHING
& associates

Table of Contents

Dedication

To Christ, above all things.

To my mom and dad for showing me Christ. To my
wife for always inspiring me.

To all who gave me ideas.

Foreword

Have you ever wondered how we got to the point we are today? How did we become so far off the mark that there seems to be no return? The culture of America has taken a downward spiral over the last few decades. That is not to say that it was ever perfect, or even close to it. But the culture has lost its way. Morality, values, and even its vision have been lost.

I teach modern world history in a public school. One major theme we always talk about is why we study history. Most of the students are coming in from middle school and have hated the last two years of history because it's just about "a bunch of dead people and facts that don't affect me." And then as the year goes by, they begin to understand that each and every action of each and every person affects each and every generation. We have a saying in my classes that to stop future mistakes from happening, you need to learn from the mistakes of the past.

It is a small passion of mine to study the differences between our generations, especially to see exactly why we are the way we are today. One of my most passionate lessons is on the counterculture of the 1960s. My students know that learning history is important.

I am only saying that because I want (not just me and my students), but everyone to look at the past and see what went wrong. Something is definitely wrong. Life is not meant to be lived the way we are living it. When God created this world and our existence, He had set up a way of life. Humans from day one, deviated from this plan and have been escalating rapidly in the past few generations even farther away from His plan.

My purpose in writing this book is that you will, hopefully, see the way God intended us to live and how He set up a system if you will, for us to follow. You will see the biblical setup of how we were supposed to function. I will try to show what God intended for all of us and how, over at least the last few decades, we have veered away from His directed path. I will try to show the breakdown and what we have become and show why we have become this way. You will begin to see the issues people have caused since we started deviating from the intended path.

This book, by the topic alone, will offend many people. This is because we all have preconceived ideas of what life is all about, and our thoughts about God. It is not meant to offend, but someone once told me that if you are satisfying everyone, you must be doing something wrong.

There is a force in today's world that is combatting the setup of God. It is called humanism. Humanism is the modern driving force behind atheism; the belief that there is no God. Humanism stresses that the intellect of mankind is the highest form of being and that the goodness of mankind is the key to solving the problems of the world. Humanism believes that the individual is the foundation of all human existence. See my book called *Charting the Three Views of God* for further explanations. In this book, you will see a piece of what humanism is, what it is doing to try to do, and how it will destroy the foundation we were set upon. You will see how humanism is not the answer to our problems but is the reason for our problems.

In the end, I hope you will see how you need to make sure you have your foundation on God, and that you choose not to follow the lies of humanism. The chart on the next page (Figure 1) might be useful, as you read some of the book. It shows the levels of atheism. Here is how you should interpret the chart. If you start at the bottom right, New Age and Harmonious ideologies are subtypes of beliefs. They are a subtype of Spiritualism. Spiritualism is a subtype of Humanism. On the bottom left, Empiricism, Utilitarianism, and Liberalism are subtypes of Secularism. Secularism is also a subtype of Humanism. Humanism is a subtype of Atheism. Again, see *Charting the Three Views of God* for more explanation. But if you can keep this chart in mind as you read, it may help understand some of the things you will read about.

Figure 1
Atheism Chart

Atheism				
Humanism				
Secularism			Spiritualism	
Liberalism	Utilitarianism	Empiricism	Harmonious	New Age

1

Structure is the Key

THE PURPOSE OF STRUCTURE

Have you ever walked into a place, like a department store, looked around for answers, and found no one to help you? There is nothing worse than not knowing what is going on around you. What makes it worse is when there is someone around, even many around you, and you still get no answers. People running around with no answers has a word for it; chaos. It is one of my biggest pet peeves. Someone needs to have the answers and should be there to help. Chaos leaves us confused and wandering through life. Chaos leaves us with more questions in life than it does with answers. The main question, in this case, is how do we get rid of chaos? We need structure. We need "order."

There is something to say about structure and order. To begin with, God gave us a structure to live by. He let us know that through the prophet Jeremiah.

Jeremiah 29:1, NIV

"For I know the plans I have for you," declares the LORD, "plans to prosper you and not to harm you, plans to give you hope and a future."

He planned to have us live under a structure. This structure would give us prosperity and hope. It would allow us to live without harm and give us something for the future. If we follow His plan, we are given this promise. All throughout His word, He has laid structure and plans for us. God's word significantly supports many scientific theories and practices as you are going to see as this book goes on. There are patterns and structures placed in our lives that help us survive. For example, imagine if the earth, the stars, and all the planets had no orbit. All the cosmological and astronomical objects that we know would be flying around space on aimless paths. Others would be sitting around hanging in space somewhere waiting for their ultimate destiny. Eventually, all the worlds would start to collide, bouncing off each other or crashing into each other like someone shaking a snow globe. That is chaos.

Both God and humans put in place systems, in order to make life easier. Take governments for example. Some have complete order and some have more freedom. Yes, democracy, and the freedom to live your life as you want, are important, and it is something to be valued. But in all honesty, even democracy still needs to have structure to remain viable as a system. The word democracy comes from two Greek words, *demos,* and *kratia.* Those words together mean "people rule." But the purest form of democracy is not perfect. If people ruled with totality, it is actually anarchy.

Anarchy is also Greek, coming from the word *anarkhia*, which is translated as "no leader." When there is no leader and no structure to leadership or society, then the people have no boundaries. Too much freedom can cause chaos, and have the adverse desired effect on what democracy is supposed to be. It would also have an adverse effect on what God wanted for us, as you will see by the end of this book. When people have no structure, society breaks down and life is not what it is supposed to be; it is perverted from the original plan. And thereby we are not living the way God intended. In this chapter, we will look at what it means to have structure in our lives and why it is important to have it.

Structure is not necessarily just all about laws and regulations, although they are many times connected. Structure instead is more about routine, expectation, and patterns. Structure in our lives adds security, stability, and serenity.

Structure allows security because, if you know what is going to happen based on routines, and you know what is supposed to happen based on expectations, then you can predict many of the things you may have to respond to. Such as, in my classes, if the students know there are rules in the classroom, then they know that if they do the right thing or the wrong thing there will be either rewards or consequences. In return, it allows the students to feel safer in class since they know there are rules and someone to enforce them. When someone acts up in class, many students want (and need) the teacher to deal with the situation. It calms them down when any disruptive behavior is de-escalated by the teacher. In the rest of society, knowing there are police officers or security guards in public places, makes people feel safer, and allows us to relax.

Structure allows stability because patterns give us consistency. Such as, when things are constant, then fewer surprises will happen. This gives the situation more momentum. Momentum helps us keep moving on the same path; hence stability. Again, students know that if there is a routine, they can expect what is next. There is less confusion about what needs to be done, and so they can keep working since they will not have to stop and rethink things. In regular life, we can see things come easier for us when we have some kind of a schedule. Time management allows us to control the flow of situations and events. The better the management, the easier life is.

"Structure" allows serenity. If you have a routine, then life becomes easier and less stressful. The lower the stress level, the more you can live with greater peace. If you know what to do, you can have more confidence in yourself and your surroundings. This allows us to have some kind of peace of mind. Elizabeth Scott, Ph.D., at Northcentral University specializes in stress management, psychology, and family counseling. She said: "Life structures can cut down our list of stressors by helping us create and maintain positive habits. This is important because habits are what drive many of the activities in our lives, whether we realize it or not." (Scott, E. 2021). We get rid of stressors by having "structure" in our lives. Having life structures can allow us to obtain peace of mind; and serenity.

We all need structure. As a teacher, the children I saw whose lives had more structure to them tended to succeed more in class. There would be higher grades, better attitudes, and they would have a more positive outlook on life. Those who had more chaos in their lives tended to miss school more, act up during class time, and they had a harder time with life lessons. They even had harder times accepting things in life. Many times, they could not even hold an actual conversation. However, those with structure even knew about timing and appropriateness of waiting for your turn and had higher listening skills. God wanted us to have structure, not to rule over us but because He knew it makes life better for us, as the passage in Jeremiah told us. So, He provided a structure for us, one with a good foundation. He is the foundation of that structure.

WHAT STRUCTURE IS NOT MEANT TO BE

Structure is not the same as controlling. Having structure is not to say that we need dictatorship or that individuals should not make their own decisions in life. That is not what I am saying at all. Look at the history of dictatorships. Dictatorships only happen when society breaks down so much that a person rises up to end the chaos. Real-life examples would be people like Napoleon of France, Benito Mussolini of Italy, Josef Stalin of the Soviet Union, Mao Zedong of China, Oliver Cromwell of England, and Adolf Hitler of Germany, just to name a few.

World War One officially ended with the Treaty of Versailles in 1919. Germany had lost the war. The Treaty, written by the Allied Powers, created a horrible situation for Germany, by forcing them to accept certain punishments. One punishment was for Germany to change their form of government. They had plunged into hyperinflation and had been sent into a stage of revolution. The new German government, called the Weimar Republic, could not handle the issues the country was dealing with. The people, piece by piece, were overthrowing them. The government was supposed to have been a democracy, but it was awful. German society had broken down. Hitler rose up among the chaos and shut it all down.

Vladimir Lenin was a believer in communism. During the First World War as well, Russia lost millions more soldiers than all the others involved. They suffered from famine and lack of supplies. Lenin took charge and started a revolution in 1917. The revolution lasted until 1922. He created a new country called the Soviet Union. However, the new Soviet Union was still chaotic, filled with more famine, economic instability, and government corruption. Lenin died in 1924, leaving controversy of leadership. Josef Stalin came in and filled the void after Lenin died. Of course, he ended up doing the same thing Lenin did, and even worse, but that just proves dictatorships never work.

England fell into a civil war in 1642 due to a power struggle between King Charles I and Parliament. From 1649 to 1653 there was a breakdown of English society. After a long bout with corrupted and incompetent kings, Oliver Cromwell overthrew the English government and tried to set up a republic. Cromwell, who was a member of Parliament, came in and set himself up as England's leader. His republic failed miserably and he became a dictator to try and stop the chaos that he helped create. Dictatorships never work.

Some fictional examples, yet very realistic all the same, would be all of the young reader books such as Suzanne Collins's *The Hunger Games*, Veronica Roth's *Divergent*, and James Dashner's *The Maze Runner* series. Even old- school books like George Orwell's *1984* and Aldous Huxley's *A Brave New World* are all good examples. All of these books show dystopian societies (a broken society turned into a controlled society) that had been created out of desperation. All the dictators in these books ended up causing more harm than good by being controlling, abusive, and oppressive. The protagonists in each book have to fight back.

Dictators only truly take over when the people are desperate or vulnerable. But structure is not about being a dictatorship. It is not about control, or abuse, or oppression. Do not get structure and these words intertwined. Structure is simply about having a strong foundation. People should choose how to live their lives, something I truly believe in, but they need a foundation to make the right choices. Individuals need a foundation. Structure gives a foundation.

WHAT STRUCTURE DOES FOR US

First of all, structure provides direction in your life. When you have direction, you "enable" and free yourself to act. Lack of direction causes indecision. When we have indecisions then anxieties, impulsive reactions, and impaired thinking may happen. These are the things that get us into trouble. We all know when we experience impaired thinking that we make the wrong decisions, and people get hurt. We all know when we have impulsive reactions, we tend to say the wrong things in an emotional way, which may cause people to be hurt as well. Anxieties cause us to panic, and turn to primitive "fight or flight" responses (Walter B. Cannon, 1915). All of these take away our decision-making skills. When we have no strong decision-making skills based on a lack of a foundation, our structure is not stable.

Things in everyday life are examples of this. Look at the stock market. The stock market is very vulnerable to speculations about what could happen. If good news about the economy happens, people feel safe with their money. If bad news comes out about money, people can panic. When people panic due to bad news and sell their stock prematurely or on impulse, or sell their stock at low prices, the stock market does not respond well to that. Go back to World War One and the signing of the Treaty of Versailles in 1919. Another punishment in the Treaty was to force Germany into giving up its military. This gave the world a sense of security. The world became relaxed. In 1929, after the world had become relaxed due to the false security of the Treaty, the world came crashing down in one day. The stock market crashed. But what led up to that? Here is a long story made short. The United States came out of WWI as a financial giant. Our fields and businesses were not destroyed by the war like they were in Europe. People knew we had the money. The world needed money to get back on its feet. People from all over the world turned to the United States to get that money. The United States' banks gave too many loans to countries like Germany. They gave loans to anyone who needed money. Countries also turned to the United States for products until they could make their own again. We overproduced because we knew people were going to buy our products out of necessity. Businesses began to over- inflate their prices and still over-produced. That is a huge "no-no" in economics if you know anything about the law of supply and demand. When you have an ample number of supplies, you keep the prices low, but the

United States kept them high. People stopped buying American products because of the high prices. Governments placed tariffs on each other to protect their own products and businesses. And then on October 29, 1929, the stock market crashed because the inflated prices fell fast. People panicked, and we went into the Great Depression. When the stocks started to fall, people did not know what to do. The stock market did not have a strong structure. These situations caused indecision and speculation. Indecisions caused widespread panic, and people ended up making impulsive decisions. Before the crash, there was no foundation to stop an event like this. After the crash, Wall Street had to put together a better structure for buying and selling, to ensure this type of economic depression would never happen again. And now we have more security, stability, and serenity (give or take a few presidents). These allow us to have direction.

Another example is in schools today. They now practice evacuation (fast exit) drills along with tornado and fire drills. Evacuation drills were established for use in case of emergencies that happen within the building, such as active shooter situations. Schools practice what to do, and one of those actions is to get out of the school as fast as possible.

One of the mottos and practices that some in educational administration use is a quote from Theodore Roosevelt, "*In any moment of decision, the best thing you can do is the right thing, the next best thing is the wrong thing, and the worst thing you can do is nothing.*" If there is indecision then many lives could be lost just due to the confusion alone. No decision means no plan of action was taken. If there is no plan then there is no structure. If there is no structure then chaos can ensue. There needs to be someone or something with direction. Structure provides that for us.

A second thing that structure does is that it allows for better communication. Businesses know the importance of structure and communication. All successful big businesses have a hierarchy of CEOs, presidents, managers, and staff. The military also knows the importance of structure for communication. Soldiers know that the chain of command needs to be followed. In both cases, there is a clear line of communication. In both cases when the hierarchy or chain of command is broken then the system breaks down and you slip into chaos. If a person skips a part of that chain, then some are left out of the loop, and will not know what to do. When a person skips part of that chain, someone who is not trusted, or perhaps should not be trusted, will be making a decision. That person may not have the experience or maybe even the intelligence to make decisions. In the end, someone or something could be hurt or destroyed. Individuals would then start making all the decisions on their own without communication. As the old saying goes, when two people feed the horse, the horse never gets fed. There need to be leaders with experience and an understanding of structure. Leaders should provide good communication. Good leaders have communication skills.

Have you ever sat in a group where all they do is discuss things and they actually never make a decision? If there is an issue, committees are created and they discuss things. If they can't make a decision they divide into other committees. Sometimes there is even a committee to discuss which committee is needed. But when that happens, communication between the committees is lost. When you have this lack of communication, then nothing is accomplished. This sounds like Congress, doesn't it? There needs to be better communication. "Structure" can give us that.

A third thing structure does is that it builds strong relationships. When you know what to expect from your partner, friend, or family member then a "trust" can start to be built. Usually, when that trust is broken, it is because that person did something wrong that you would never have expected them to do. Relationships cannot be built on spur- of-the-moment decisions. Reality shows are horrible. Reality shows that try to create relationships are the worst. These relationships are artificial and superficial. No one should marry anyone the first time they see them. Ninety days may not even be enough time to determine whether to marry someone. Giving someone a rose does not mean perfect love. Neither person knows what to really expect from the other. So, they are forced to start to know each other without anything to stand upon. Like a foundation without structure, that marriage will not last, and you see the pain brought on by the sudden break-up. But I guess at least you have a good television show to watch if you want the drama. Relationships need a foundation.

A fourth thing structure does is that it allows you to become good at the things in your life. As we said earlier, structure adds routine to your life. Routines can cause habits, and habits can become lifestyles over time. As stated before, "Life structures can cut down our list of stressors by helping us create and maintain positive habits. This is important because habits are what drive many of the activities in our lives." (Elizabeth Scott, 2021) Positive, or good habits are good for your life. Good habits can drive your life in a good direction. When you have good structure, and you know what to expect in life, it adds confidence which allows you to have more motivation. Routines allow you to do things with fewer chances of doing them wrong. A good foundation allows you to have and do good things in life.

WHY THE INDIVIDUAL NEEDS STRUCTURE

The individual needs structure. The individual needs a strong foundation to stand on to make sure the structure will last. Now, of course, you do not want bad, or negative, habits developing to where your life becomes miserable, but that will help prove my points. One needs a good foundation so the structure has something to stand on that causes good and positive habits that allow a good life.

Not to make light of this at all, but those who have autism have an easier time when there are patterns. They function better and it calms them down. Laurent Mottron of the Centre for Excellence in Pervasive Development Disorders at the University of Montreal said, in an interview a few years ago: "For example, many people with autism have hyperlexia, which is characterized by above-average abilities in reading and decoding language, but poor abilities in reading comprehension. Instead of using punishment or reinforcement to teach people with hyperlexia, it would be better to teach them by introducing letters as **families of patterns** so they can better understand written materials." (Laurent Mottron, 2013). Patterns seem to be a basis of existence and helpful to all.

The main point trying to be made here is that people need some kind of structure. Without structure, the human race would be unstable. But a structure needs a good foundation. If a structure is built upon the wrong foundation, then that structure would still be unstable. It reminds me of what Jesus said about which foundation you are building your house upon in the book of Matthew.

Matthew 7:27, NCV

"Everyone who hears my words and obeys them is like a wise man who built his house on rock. It rained hard, the floods came, and the winds blew and hit that house. But it did not fall, because it was built on rock. Everyone who hears my words and does not obey them is like a foolish man who built his house on sand. It rained hard, the floods came, and the winds blew and hit that house, and it fell with a big crash."

You can either build it on the sand (unstable) or build it on the "rock" (stable). Our foundation needs to be on the "rock" but the world, unfortunately, has rebuilt it on the sand and they don't even know they did. If you are not on a solid foundation, a crash is waiting to happen. God is that needed foundation.

A GODLY FOUNDATION

Figure 2
A Godly Foundation

| **Individual** |
| Beliefs (relations) and actions (responsibility) |
| **Culture** |
| Laws of man, mores, customs/traditions, groups |
| **Family** |
| Love, honor, sharing, teaching, values |
| **GOD** |
| Creation, universal laws, moral standards |

Above (Figure 2) is the structure we should build with, and the foundation we should build our lives on. The chart is Biblical, arguably scientific, and uses common sense. The Bible specifically talks about these and the importance each one plays in our existence. The world will disagree with this structure, but you will see later why they would be wrong, and why it would be wrong to do anything else.

At the bottom is the foundation, God. Everything is built upon Him. Each step adds influence to the step above it. The individual is in charge of his or her own beliefs and actions. The results of their actions create our history and drive our future. The individual builds relations based on his or her beliefs. Our beliefs and actions are a result of the structure and foundation they are built upon. Our beliefs allow us to find relationships. The individual builds friendships when they find someone like them and who they have something in common with. Most of the common issues are our beliefs. They fall in love with someone who may share their common dreams, desires, and values. The individual is responsible for his or her actions. The individual is bound though, by the other three parts of the structure underneath them.

We have to work and act within our culture. There are laws that we have to respect, and our actions are held accountable to those laws. There are values taught by the family that we hold dear, and that help us build our relationships. And then there are moral standards the individual cannot throw away; laid down by God. The world will try and tell us that there is no one standard we all have to abide by. Whatever is right for you may not be right for me. **No. That is a humanist lie.**

Our culture is not a foundation. Our customs and traditions stem from families over the generations of time. Our culture is built by families who have bonded together over time to teach right from wrong. Many times, throughout history that is how we developed a system of our laws. Laws developed out of community values and standards. But those standards had a beginning place. Those things we are supposed to teach as right from wrong come from the standards that God had put into place. Why is He able to set these standards? Because He is the Creator.

Family is the strongest unit. But the family is still not the foundation. That unit is built upon the love that God shows and describes throughout His holy word.

In the end, God is the foundation of our existence.

How is *this* structure in Figure 2 biblically based? Obviously, the foundation is what God wanted. He wanted all of us to rely upon Him, and place our trust in Him. He wanted us to have a relationship with Him no matter what we did with our lives. The family was the first thing that God instituted after all life was created. We find that in Genesis.

Genesis 2:18-24, (NLT)

"Then the Lord God said, "It is not good for the man to be alone. I will make a helper who is just right for him." So the Lord God formed from the ground all the wild animals and all the birds of the sky. He brought them to the man to see what he would call them, and the man chose a name for each one. He gave names to all the livestock, all the birds of the sky, and all the wild animals. But still, there was no helper just right for him. So the Lord God caused the man to fall into a deep sleep. While the man slept, the Lord God took out one of the man's ribs and closed up the opening. Then the Lord God made a woman from the rib, and he brought her to the man. "At last!" the man exclaimed. "This one is bone from my bone and flesh from my flesh! She will be called 'woman,' because she was taken from 'man.'" This explains why a man leaves his father and mother and is joined to his wife, and the two are united into one."

Reflect on this for a few moments. God said it was not good for man to be alone. He created a suitable helper for him. He created one not out of the bones of the head, so man would not be overruled by the helper. He did not create one out of the feet, so man would not overrule that helper. He created one out of the ribs; so that they can be side by side. He created a helper, not a slave. When Adam saw this, he knew she was from him and was now part of him. And it was a woman. God then gave them to each other and the family was started.

Genesis 1:28, (NIV)

*God blessed them and said to them, "Be **fruitful and increase** in number; fill the earth and **subdue** it. Rule over the fish in the sea and the birds in the sky and over every living creature that moves on the ground."*

After the family was created, He gave Adam and Eve a responsibility. They were supposed to be fruitful and increase in number. This is the second sign of a family. They were to increase in numbers, creating a family. They were supposed to fill the earth. If they filled the earth this means many people, a culture if you will, would be created over time. But look at what it says right after "fill the earth." It says man was supposed to subdue the earth. The Hebrew word for subdue is *kavash*. This word means to bring into submission. That does not mean ruling over with a harsh iron fist. Submission actually means peaceful and tender obedience. In other words, man was not supposed to live in turmoil and hate or oppress anything. People were supposed to live as one and together. They would grow into a community; a culture. This culture would be built upon the family and the family would be grounded on the foundation of God.

The individual is part of the structure because each and every one of us is supposed to have a relationship with the other three, ultimately with God. The individual is part of the culture. The individual is part of a family. And the individual is part of God. Keep in mind that the individual is self-responsible as well. So, even though we are part of this structure we are supposed to make sure our lives are being lived right and according to His word.

Scientifically, we were meant to live by structure. The world knows that. Socially, this is why we have laws and government. This is why we have ways of life. This is why we even have laws of nature. Isaac Newton and others discovered there were patterns in our physical world that we are bound by. Motion, gravity, thermodynamics, and so forth, are things we cannot change. The circle of life is a scientific pattern. Our whole existence is based on structure. Patterns and structures are seen in physics, chemistry, biology, and psychiatry. David E. Morrison, M.D. of Psychiatry from the Menninger Foundation, is now a consultant and the founder of Morrison Associates, Ltd. He has been an expert in the field of executive and organizational development since the mid-1990s. He said: "Humans depend upon structure to comprehend their experience. The sources and functions of structure are so ubiquitous that most people don't know they need them until they are gone. This need for structure is an important cause of resistance to change. Understanding the role of structure for human equilibrium is an important part of building a strategy to manage the otherwise confusing human responses to change." (David Morrison, 1995). Basically, he is saying that structure eases confusion and allows us to comprehend our surroundings more easily. In other words, it is nature's way of *plans to prosper you and not to harm you, plans to give you hope and a future.*

Patricia Duggan, Post-Graduate Diploma in CBT from the University of West of Scotland, winner of multiple awards in the field of cognitive behavior therapy said: "Human beings need structure and routine. It is a basic need, particularly for children. Without that structure, we feel uncertain and chaotic, and for children, this can feel void of control and predictability." (Patricia Duggan, 2020). She agrees that without structure, we lose the psychological security of the routine, or the stability discussed earlier. Having structure is a basic need of human beings. Something laid down by God.

Structure is the key to having a strong foundation. We need to have the right foundation.

God is that foundation.

God?

2
God is the Foundation

GOD IS THE CREATOR

Is God real? This question is the most essential question of the human race. If there isn't a God, nothing really matters, all existence has no purpose. But if there is a God then He has to be the beginning of it all, and therefore has to be the foundation for everything.

As a teacher, sometimes I joke with my students about their extracurricular activities; mostly soccer players and cheerleaders. I say things like "Soccer is just running back and forth with one person kicking a ball." Or I say "Cheerleading isn't a sport". But I say that mostly with tongue in cheek. I did get to watch cheerleading championships at the school I teach, and I was impressed with the athleticism. The cliché position of cheerleading is the pyramid. It is a simple move, but it still needs to be done delicately and designed correctly. You most certainly do not want to put the smallest of the group at the bottom, or line up with the most uneven sizes to hold the rest of the pyramid up. In other words, you have to pick the right base for the best foundation.

Being the foundation means you or some item has to be the strongest to be the first of a structure. God is not only the strongest but is also the first of life's structure. How can He be both? He is both because He is the Creator of all existence. This is something non-believers, especially those who believe in humanism or believe that science is nature's god, cannot grasp. Humanists, atheists, and liberals cannot accept that God is the foundation because they do not believe He exists. But God is the one and only Creator. He created scientific laws and laws of nature. He even allows science to explain *His* existence. The Bible shows this science and shows how He is the foundation by being the Creator. This chapter will show how God exists, using some science, experience, and common sense, and why He is the foundation.

When God created our existence, He set into place all that we know. He created what we call scientific laws and universal statements like gravity and thermodynamics. He created mathematical patterns all around us like "pi" and the degrees of all shapes. He put into place all we can see, all we can hear, all we can touch, and all of the things we cannot. But we have to have a starting point. The universe has to have some basis to begin with.

There are four components that the universe started with to make that basis. He created the four components of the universe. These components are space, time, matter, and energy. All of our universe is known to be composed of those four components. He set up natural and universal laws such as gravity, motion, sound, and such. He put them into place, all within the compounds of these components. And when He set these up, He also set up one major foundation, Himself. He is the foundation of all of our existence.

From the very first verse in the Bible, Him being the foundation is made clear. When Genesis 1:1 says, "In the beginning, God created," it says all we need to know. God did it all. It shows where we came from, and how we were created, and it gives us an actual timeline of when we were created (although that part leaves many theories to be studied). Let's take a deeper look at the whole passage because there is more to it than what we see.

GENESIS- THE BEGINNING OF EVERYTHING

The word Genesis means "beginnings." Genesis tells us the story of our creation and lays the groundwork to show that God is the foundation from the beginning. He is the Creator. "*In the beginning, God created the heavens and the earth.*" We all know the passage but what does it really mean? Before we can comprehend it, we must look at the original language as much as possible. The word of God has meaning and purpose. There is not one thing in the Bible that is written just to take up space. I believe that the original message of the Bible is infallible but I also believe that the differences in languages and translations leave priorities out. I once had a five-year argument with a person in the Australia/New Zealand region about the language of the Bible. He claimed that the Bible was originally written in English. He said God spoke to Adam in English. And therefore, only English should be used to interpret what God has said. Yes, that is what he said. Adam knew English somehow 3000 years before the English language was created. There are so many things wrong with that statement.

But even if the Bible was written in English, then it still leaves a lot out of what we could know. That is not to say the English versions are wrong; not at all. *"In the beginning, God created the heavens and the earth"* is 100% accurate and reliable. But if we read it in Hebrew, as it was originally written, then we can see more of the mind of God. We can get more of the truth and see how there is no other way to explain our existence unless there is a God who created it. As I stated earlier, every word and even every letter of God's word has a purpose. In Hebrew, letters have meanings and not just sounds. Such as in the United States we have a nursery rhyme that goes, "A" is for apple. It really doesn't mean that but it is a way for young children to learn their alphabet and phonics. But in Hebrew letters really do have actual meanings. The letter "A" in Hebrew is pronounced *aleph* and it has the meaning of a bull, or strong, or head (in charge). For more detail about the Hebrew alphabet and the meanings of the letters (See resource page). With that said, look at the first verse in the Bible, the story of creation, in the original Hebrew. It shows the connection with God being the foundation.

In Hebrew, the passage in Genesis 1:1 reads,

"B'resheet bara Elohim 'et hashamayim v'et ha'aretz".

There are different ways to spell some of these words depending on the style. For example, *B'resheet* can also be spelled *bereshit*. You will see why I said that in a few moments. The first word in the whole Bible is *b'resheet*. We translate that into English as "in the beginning," but there is so much more hidden, if you will, in the phrase. The first two letters of that word in Hebrew are *bet* (b) and *resh (r)*. Remember, letters in Hebrew have meaning. *Bet* means house and *resh* means head. Put them together and you get the Hebrew word *bar*. *Bar* in Hebrew is translated as "son." This type of son means head of the household such as what the firstborn son would be considered. This is the first thing the Bible says. The Son (Jesus) is at the beginning of Creation. He was in control, the head of creation. He is the Creator. He was there before the world began as part of the Trinity. He is the foundation. This calls to mind what John said at the beginning of his gospel.

John 1:1-3, (NASB)

*"In the beginning was the Word, and the Word was **with** God, and the Word **was** God. He was in the beginning with God. All things came into being **through** Him, and apart from Him **nothing** came into being that has come into being."*

Jesus, the Son, the head of all creation, was with God in the beginning. This next part is a hard concept for non- believers---He also *was* God in the beginning as part of the Trinity aforementioned. It's an easy concept actually. Think of an egg. You have the shell, the yolk, and the albumen, but it's all still considered an egg. Nothing that we know was created without Jesus. Jesus is God. God is the foundation of all things.

Now let's go back to the English words and study exactly what they mean, and why we need to know them. What does "in the beginning" mean? In the beginning of what? The word "beginning" means the start of something. What had started? Our existence started. When God started this creation, our whole existence came into being. The existence of everything started right then and there.

We started to exist. Time started to exist. Our clock started to tick. The time of mankind began. Time; a component of the universe was created. God created time. God is the Creator.

What was the next step in time? All of a sudden, we have creation, not just a piece of it, but all of it, all at once. Science claims there was a Big Bang and so does God. The second word from Genesis 1:1 in Hebrew is "*bara*". The translation of *bara* is "creating out of nothing." There are those who will argue this point. Many will try to say that *bara* means "making something out of something that already exists" like when someone makes a desk out of lumber. But they are getting the word confused with *asah. Bara* is clearly used here and so it stands that God created all that we know out of nothing and not out of something that already existed. You will see why that statement is important a little later. All of a sudden! All that we know came from nothing. Think about that. What was here before anything in our physical universe? Absolutely nothing! God even had to create a place that would hold our universe. He created a whole new plane of existence. That is power. Science is correct. There was a "big bang." Not one due to an accident, but one done with a purpose. If there is a purpose, then someone had to have done it, otherwise, it was still an accident. That will also be discussed later. God was the one who created everything with purpose. God is the Creator.

The third word from Genesis 1:1 in Hebrew, says Elohim is the one who did it. The word *El* means God. El is sometimes added to the ending of names to show a connection with God. This is where we get names like Gabri'el, Ezeki'el, and Micha'el. Gabri'el means "God is my strength." Ezeki'el means "God is strong.'. The name Micha'el in Hebrew means "one who is like God.'. This is why the "e" comes after the "a" in Michael when we spell it in English; something that always bothered me as a child. I never could understand why it wasn't spelled Micheal, but now I do. These names that are mentioned, and a few others like them all have something to do with God. There is more to Elohim though, even more than just a name. When you see "*im*" at the end of a Hebrew noun it means it is plural, such as cherub means one angel but cherubim means more than one. It is the equivalent of the "s" in English. This is not to say that God is more than one or polytheistic like many atheists try to claim Christians worship. The verb *bara* that we just looked at is in the singular form. If the verb here was plural, the word would have been "*baru*", but it is not. God is singular. So why is it written in plural form but with a singular verb? This is the first sign of a Trinity. Jesus was with God, and Jesus was God as we stated earlier. There are three personas, but they are One. Genesis adds in the very next verse:

Genesis 1:2, (Berean Study Bible)

*"Now the earth was formless and void, and darkness was over the surface of the deep. And the **Spirit of God** was hovering over the surface of the waters."*

The Spirit was there too in the beginning, thereby making Him equivalent to God as well, the third part of the Trinity. Nothing else or persona of God was mentioned. There were only three mentioned and these three are One. This is complementary to what was written in Deuteronomy, and we see this being further accurate:

Deuteronomy 6:4, (KJV)

"Hear, O Israel: The Lord (Adonai) our God (Eloheinu), the Lord is one!"

Eloheinu is a form of *Elohim*. God, the Trinity, created all that we know. Why would this passage have to show God is One but also in a plural form? It says it because of the concept of the Trinity. Scripture is filled with references to a Trinity. Such as, later on, in Genesis, it says:

Genesis 1:26, (LEB).

*"And God said, "Let **us** make humankind in our image and according to **our** likeness."*

Notice the plurality. They were all together at this point. There is one more point in this passage I just found. The word "make" here in Hebrew is *asah*. Remember what I said earlier? That word means to make something out of something else. Humankind is created in the likeness of Him. Something was given to us that nothing else in creation has; a spirit. We as humans were not made out of nothing. We were made from Him, a part of Him. We were given a spirit. We were made to be of Him. He is supposed to be part of us. He is the Creator. He is the foundation.

We will skip the fourth word for now. Trust me. I will return to it because it is the most important word in this whole passage!

The fifth word is *hashamayim*, the heavens. The next step after the creation of time was the creation of the heavens. But what is "the heavens"? Most people probably think this means Heaven as opposed to just the earth but that is not what it means. It is better translated as space, or above the earth. Notice the "im" at the end of *hashamayim*. This word is plural. Even in English, it has an "s" on the end so it can't just mean one place such as Heaven itself. But space is one, so why would it be plural? The root word is *mayim* which is the Hebrew word for water. There was water on the Earth. There was water in the sky. There was water in the atmosphere. Water could also be translated as "the deep" or "the dark". Anything above the dry land of the Earth was and will be considered "water." Anything above the land would be considered space, the deep, the dark. Hence *hashamayim* is space and all of it that it entails, plural. Space; a component of the universe was created. God is real and the Creator.

The sixth word simply means "and"; *v'et*. This could mean that it is just a conjunction that connects two or more objects, or it could mean that the two terms on either side are the same item. Such as we can say baseball *and* basketball. They both are games but are not really connected. We can also say ham *and* eggs. They are separate items but the same meal and are connected. The word "and" has more power than we give credit. Either way, the word *v'et* works in both scenarios here. You will again see why this is important later. God is real AND the Creator. God is the foundation.

The seventh word of the phrase is *ha'aretz*. That simply means earth, or the land, as in one piece. Notice it is not plural. Land is anything that is solid or with the ability to become solid. At first, the earth was formless but took shape, and then land appeared. Land is a place of elements or matter. Matter; a third component of the universe was created. God is real and the Creator. God is the foundation. Are you getting it yet?

Now let's go back to the word I skipped. As I said this is the most important word used in this whole passage. The word I typed is "*et*." It is not the same as *v'et* which is a completely different word. If we actually used the original Hebrew sounds and letters and then translated them into English, we get the letter "A" and the letter "T." Some Hebrew translations have this word as "*at*" and not "et" in the scripture. It's the same word either way. It's kind of like grey and gray. It is the same word but a different spelling. Now, do you see why I said you could spell things differently and why it was important to know? Those two letters are very important. "A" in Hebrew is *aleph* and "T" in Hebrew is *tav*. Rabbi Chaim Weiner said: "The word את [et] is the most frequent word in Hebrew. It constitutes over 2% of the words in any text – making it more than twice as frequent as the next word on the list. And it doesn't even mean anything." (Chaim Weiner, 2014). This word is the second most used word in Hebrew, but there is no direct translation of the word. It has no meaning, or so they think. Most Jewish people do not even know what it means. They are two letters that do not spell anything in their language when put together alone, yet they use it all the time. *Aleph* and *Tav* are the first letter and last letter of the Hebrew alphabet. Even if we put our first and last letters (A and Z) together, it is not a word for us either (even though this is just a coincidence, it is a good example). But we don't go around saying "az" 2% of the time right in the middle of our sentences. Why are these two letters important, and even more so, why are they combined? Let's make it even more interesting before we look at the reason. The Greeks' first and last letters are *alpha* and *omega*. Ok. Here we go. Jesus said, "I am the Alpha and the Omega -- the Beginning and End -- the First and the Last." (Revelation 22:13, YLT) Jesus is the Alpha AND Omega. Jesus is the *Aleph* AND *Tav*. The "and" here connects them as One! He is the beginning and the end at the same time. He has always been here. He is. God told Moses to tell the people that "I AM" sent him. He is the great "I AM". That is the same thing. I told you I would come back to that. The opening verses in Genesis that we have been looking at, have now been connected as well. That middle word, the fourth word, is "*et*", the *aleph*, and *tav*. Jesus is not only the Creator at the beginning, but He is also in the middle of all creation, meaning it was done by His design. There is one more major connection, and then I will move on. Revelation says Jesus is the beginning and the end. Is He? The very first letter of the Bible is *"bet"* as we have stated before. The last letter in the whole Bible is *"nun."* In English, the last word is "amen" (from the Hebrew word *amein*) making "n" the last letter of the Bible. When you put *bet* and *nun* together, you get the Hebrew word *bin*, another word meaning Son! Jesus is the Son and He is the beginning and the end. He is the Creator. He is God. And son here, by the way, means "heir." He is the head of the house in the beginning, and He is the heir to the throne in the end. He is the foundation of all we know and of all we are. Those who speak Hebrew, unfortunately, do not realize they are speaking of Jesus 2% of the time. God is real and the Creator. God is the foundation.

So now we have three of the four components in place. We have time, space, and matter. The universe was set and ready to go. We needed one more component for creation to be complete. The last component is energy. After the other three components were put into place, all other things were now able to come into existence. The potential of all life was ready. What needed to come next, was to transfer or convert this potential energy into kinetic energy. Isaac Newton's First Law of Thermodynamics states that energy can neither be created nor destroyed; energy can only be transferred or changed from one form to another. Well, it had to come from somewhere. After matter and space were created, the universe had the potential to convert energy. Is that mentioned in the Bible? Read the third verse in Genesis.

Genesis 1:3, (KJV)

"And God said, 'Let there be light': and there was light."

Matter was spread throughout the universe in the big bang, and a lot of it was converted to energy at the speed of light. As matter rushed from one end of the universe to the other, it created kinetic energy. Light (a form of energy) was available. Matter can be converted into energy by annihilation, fission, and fusion. Annihilation is when two or more particles collide, disappear, and release energy. Fission is when particles divide. Fusions are when two or more particles join together. Einstein's theory of relativity says that E=mc2. "E" is energy and "M" is matter. They are directly proportional. "C" stands for the speed of light. Look how it fits with what I said. At the speed of light, matter and energy converged. When one changed, so did the other. Matter had converted into energy. Read more about the theory, and you will see how God said it first. Einstein was a genius. God is even smarter. Genesis explains the basic foundation of all life. It lays the foundation for the laws of physics. God is the foundation, but as stated at the beginning of this chapter humanists, atheists, and many liberals cannot and will not accept this. They will try to prove that God is not the foundation, nor even real. They will try to destroy this foundation. And that will, in the end, destroy the structure we were meant to have. To have structure, you have to have a place to begin; where it all came together. So, what do scientists say about our beginnings?

SCIENCE AND THE BEGINNING

There's an old joke about scientific arrogance. One day a group of scientists got together, and decided that humanity had come a long way, and no longer needed God. So, they went to tell Him that they were done with Him. They walked up to God and said, "God, we've decided that we no longer need you. We have come so far like traveling in space, discovering laws of nature, and many other miraculous things. We even have cloned humans, and now can create our own humans. So why don't you just go away and mind your own business from now on?" God listened very patiently and kindly to them. After the scientists were done talking, God said, "Very well. I will go. Before I go, let's have a human-making contest." To which the scientists replied, "Okay, we can handle that!" "But," God added, "we're going to do this just like I did back in the old days with Adam." The scientists nodded, "Sure, no problem" and bent down and picked up a handful of dirt. God wagged a finger at them and said, "No. No. No. Put that down. Get your own dirt."

The one thing science really wants to discover is the beginning of life. There is constantly some study that tries to find the beginnings of the universe. Carl Sagan is known to have said, "To really make an apple pie from scratch, you must begin by inventing the universe." It's the question that haunts us all. All the things that point to God as a Creator, but for some reason, many scientists will not accept all that has been discussed so far. We know what creates life as in reproduction. We have the basic blocks of life as in DNA. We know what is needed for life to occur. But they just can't find the actual beginning. They need to keep looking for their answer. So, they turn to science to develop theories of our beginnings.

The most common theory of course is the Big Bang Theory. But since science is incomplete, there have to be studies to try to fill the voids in the explanation. Such as, in the scientific version of the Big Bang Theory, there are a few problems with how the universe expanded over time.

NASA's Wilkinson Microwave Anisotropy Probe (WMAP) was a mission by NASA that was launched in the summer of 2001 to study the properties of our universe. The information discovered with this probe seemingly answered the problems of the Big Bang Theory. WMAP has shown the universe to be basically flat. But one idea from the Big Bang Theory is that the universe was curved and grew with time. NASA claims "a universe as flat as we see it today would require an extreme fine-tuning of conditions in the past, which would be an unbelievable coincidence." (See resource page) What fine-tuned it? Coincidence? We know the actual answer.

One major theory of physics is cosmic inflation, developed by Alan Guth, Andrei Linde, Paul Steinhardt, and Andy Albrecht. This theory answers the issues the WMAP found.

In very short terms, this theory states that there was an expansion of the universe 10-36 seconds after the Big Bang (creation) and lasted until 10-32 seconds after the Big Bang. That is 10 divided by 10, 36 times when it all started, and 10 divided by 10, 32 times when the expansion ended. That is fast! That is faster than blinking since blinking is 10-4 seconds. So, the whole universe started faster than you can blink. And then expanded very fast. But then apparently, continually expanded at a much slower pace.

Most scientific studies say the expansion has now slowed down, especially lately, within the last 13 billion years. They call this the inflationary period. Then after this expansion, there was a period of darkness known as the Dark Ages, not to be confused with the historical Dark Ages that encompasses the period between the fall of the Roman Empire and the Renaissance. Inflation answers the flatness problem by saying the universe has expanded so much that from our perspective it seems flat. Such as, we all know the world is round, but it sure looks flat standing where we are. Now imagine the size of the universe in the same way. We couldn't see the curve since it was too far away to see. But it was still "fine-tuned" in the beginning.

Figure 3
WMAP

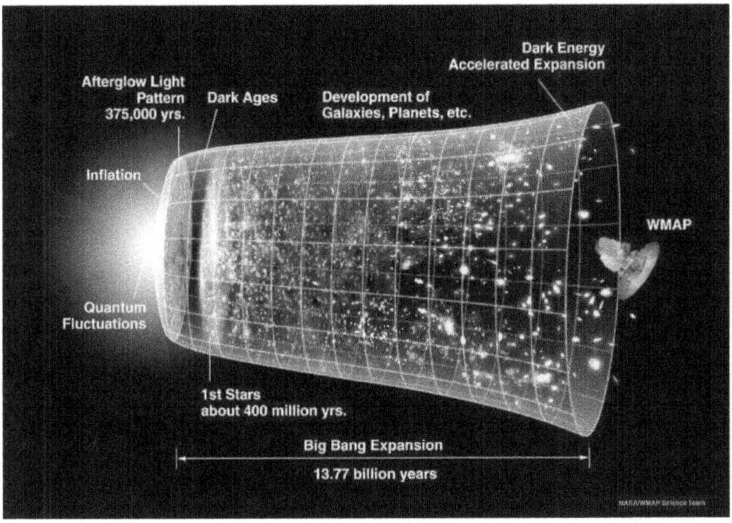

Source: NASA.gov Credit: NASA / WMAP Science Team Timeline of the Universe image. (n.d.).
https://map.gsfc.nasa.gov/media/060915/index.html

Another issue of the Big Bang Theory is that the universe could not have started at the same point because the distance between them exceeds the amount of time needed for light to travel with them. But the temperature readings prove they had to have been in contact with each other. Their answer for this is that things were actually much closer together prior to inflation than they would have been with only the original Big Bang expansion theory. In this explanation, regions could have been in causal contact prior to Inflation and could have attained a uniform temperature. Sounds like an excuse. There is a better explanation and one easier to understand. Go back to Genesis 1:1-3. Light was created AFTER all the matter. Light would not be reaching the same distance since it was created a little later.

Figure 3 shows a representation of the mission. You can see the satellite/probe on the right known as WMAP. It is trying to show that it has mapped data of the universe, starting from the Big Bang up until now. It is showing the concepts of the expansion, Dark Ages, inflation, and quantum fluctuations, and when they happened. Expansion is easy to understand. It is just referring to how the universe expanded. Inflation is just a term they use for the beginning of expansion, i.e., at the time of the Big Bang. The Dark Ages was a time period when light was trapped by some hydrogen fog in space. "Light" had to be released from the trap. Quantum fluctuations are when there are changes in energy levels. I personally love this diagram because it is scientific and biblical at the same time.

How is it biblical? Genesis 1:1 says that out of nothing, all was created. Go back to Chapter 2, and reread the section about the word "bara". There was nothing, and then there was everything. Sounds like a big bang, doesn't it? Notice there is a definite beginning on the chart in Figure 3, otherwise known as time. Then comes space and matter as already discussed. Then science said there is a flash of light that happens a little later. All of that was before the earth itself was formed. Now, go back to Verse 2 in Genesis 1 and notice the Bible says the earth was formless and darkness covered the waters. This time of darkness that the Bible mentions is the same Dark Ages that science claims. Both science and the Bible say there was a time of darkness. Quantum fluctuations happen and those are small changes that involve transferring particles of energy. Well, after this dark period, there came a time of quantum fluctuations that started up again and have remained ever since. There was a change in energy levels and cosmic inflation, and then came what is called the afterglow, which is the radiation left behind by all of this. All of this coincides with what the Bible says, "Let there be light." And notice it didn't happen in Verse 1 or 2. It happened later. Science says light came later. So does the Bible. Matter had been converted into energy-light.

I have added my own chart to make a comparison to what science says, and to what the Bible says about when things were created. Notice they both have the same progression of events. There was a fast creation (big bang). There was a small amount of time after the creation of space and matter (darkness) and light (afterglow). Then came the transference of light and the conversion of matter into energy (quantum fluctuations).

Figure 4
Bible/Science Timelines Compared

	Genesis 1:1		Genesis 1:2	Genesis 1:3	
Bible Timeline	10^{-36} seconds		10^{-32} seconds		
	Time, Space, Matter		Darkness	Light--------→Energy	
	Big Bang Expansion		Dark Ages	After Glow	Quantum Fluctuations
Science Timeline	10^{-36} seconds	10^{-32} seconds	13 billion years	375,000 years	

Source: Personal vision comparing scientific and biblical timelines.

Most of the scientific theories out there claim that all of this took 13 billion years or more. However, if things at the beginning of the Big Bang moved so fast at first, then why would the rest of it take so long? The answer is, it didn't. Go back to Einstein's theory. They change at the same rate! I believe what science found is actually quite accurate, all except for the slowing down at the miserable speed of 13 billion years. It all took less than a second. Science says it couldn't have happened that fast since we can see light from 13 billion light-years away. This Biblical theory I have listed here explains why we can see things like the light from stars that are billions of light-years away. It all happened at once, everywhere. The light has always been here because it was all created at once. It wouldn't and didn't take 13 billion years if it was all done at once. It was "matter" that had been converted to energy (light) that had been here since the beginning of time, creation.

He is the foundation. He is the Creator.

SCIENTIFIC ALTERNATIVES

If God is not the Creator, then He cannot be the foundation. If that is true, then there must be an alternative. What can the alternatives be? Could all creation/the beginning just be done by nature? Think about it. How can something that is not alive or sentient create anything? Evolutionists claim that nature selects all changes of life. How can nature have created, or at least be in control of all of these, especially if all of what we know is an accident or just some random cosmic event? How can all of this be random, and still work with so many structured laws of the universe? If there are laws, wouldn't that suggest that those laws are there with a purpose? And if there is a purpose, wouldn't that also suggest something had a reason for giving it all a purpose? Nature has laws, and picks species to change right? If nature had that power, and could control the changes and events of the universe and ALL that is in existence, then nature is God (sarcasm). In essence, that is what atheists are saying. If all of this is done naturally or driven by nature, then nature is in control, hence a god. Atheists will claim that is not what they are saying, but they know it to be true at that point. They couldn't agree out loud, because it would give a basis for some kind of god, whether that be nature or God above. But that is what they are saying.

God created those physical laws for us to be bound by, to give us some structure. No physical law can be broken by people or nature without a miracle. All laws are consistent. Whatever goes up must come down. Any object in motion remains in motion until something gets in its way. There are only three primary colors, and all other colors stem from these three. The speed of light is constant. If things are consistent and not able to be broken, then that means the laws are set. They can never be changed. Something is keeping them constant. They are being held together. They must have been made that way. Was it nature? Does nature really have that much power? No. God made the laws. God holds all of these laws together.

Colossians 1:17, (NLT)

*"He existed **before** anything else, and he **holds** all creation together."*

When you add the passages from John already stated about Him being there in the beginning, the consistency is beyond many comprehensions and the odds. There is a reason why math, physics, chemistry, biology, and patterns all have laws, theorems, systems, and properties. God created them. God made them consistent. God holds them together. God is the foundation. Are you getting it yet?

Could all of this just have been an accident? Use common sense here. How can all of what we know come from an accident, some random event with no purpose? How can life in all of its complexities, come from some primordial soup that has no sentience within it? How can some primordial soup, that would become all that we know, come from nothing? And if it was an accident, then why or how would there be any order that would follow? This is where atheists come up with excuses. If they can show an alternative to our beginnings, then the probability of God becomes less. But listen to their alternatives and see if you can agree if mankind with humanistic ideas is the foundation of our existence, or if God is. Keep in mind there are many more than these that I have listed.

They will say we came from another universe since the first law of thermodynamics says energy cannot be created only transferred. One such theory is called the Conformal Cyclic Model (Roger Penrose, 2010).

It basically says that our universe came from a big bang that was started by another universe that was here before ours. That universe came from another big bang from another universe before it. There have been infinite cycles of this. All universes come from another universe before it. Problem; where did that universe come from? And then where did the one come before that, and the one before that? There had to be a first, right? How can this be infinite?

They might say we may be just a hologram. This is called the Holographic Principle (Leonard Susskind, 2004). I had a hard time reading about this one. The theory proposes that our universe is a three- dimensional image projected off a two-dimensional surface. That sentence alone is confusing. It was a major headache trying to read about it, because they said for this to even happen, the laws of physics need to be changed, or have two sets of laws to choose from to be consistent, or to explain what is happening in our world. Wow. Anyway, here is the bigger problem; who created the hologram or even the two- dimensional surface? Even more, who is watching the hologram? Why was the hologram created? This theory also says that all we know is just an illusion. Understand? According to this theory, you are not real. You are just an illusion. You have no purpose. If you have no purpose and are not real then how did we figure out the answer to begin with? It kind of makes you feel special, doesn't it?

They might say we are a result of some electromagnetic process, such as a theory called Plasma Universe Theory (Hannes Alfvén, 1981). We were formed by some magnetic process. Plasma, which is electrically charged, in forms like the sun, auroras, and nebulas moves throughout the universe pulling things together through electromagnetism and not by gravity. Problem; how did plasma and any electromagnetism get here?

And then they even have one that states, the universe has always been here called the Steady State Theory (Fred Hoyle, Hermann Bondi, and Thomas Gold, 1948). This theory states that all we see in the universe has remained the same regardless of time or place. That is the opposite of the Big Bang Theory. In this theory, everything has always been here. But then ask these people about

God being a creator, and they will argue that if God created all of this then who created Him? They have no issue with the universe being infinite, but they have all kinds of issues with a Supreme Being existing as infinite.

See the pattern? All of their theories state a way of getting here or staying here, but something had to put all of that into motion unless this *is* all an accident. But again, how could all of this just be an accident with so many patterns and constants? And keep in mind all of the theories mentioned are in opposition, or have a contradiction to each other in some way or somehow, hence why they are only theories. But God is consistent. God created the patterns with a purpose. God is the foundation.

THE FOUNDATION IS MORALLY SET

Now that we see, or at least should be open to the idea, that God has created all things, and has laid down everything for us, there is one more thing we have to look at. God also set up a moral system. This is something atheists get upset with to the extreme. Their biggest argument here is "Which morality system is the right one?" Or they will say that morality is "subjective." These are two very common arguments that I personally have had with atheists, especially those specialist professional all-knowing scientific intellects that are found on internet forums. There can be nothing further from the truth of the second argument. First, there is only one morality system and that is the one God set up. If He is the Creator then His laws do matter and are "truth." And it's not even technically the Ten Commandments I am referring to. Those were written down 2000 years after the fall of man. The original morality system was to live in Paradise, living the perfect life, walking with Him and having a relationship with Him; getting to do anything, but eating from one tree. That was it. Don't eat from ONE tree. We were supposed to have a perfect relationship with Him. He created a perfect system. But we threw away that system by eating from the Tree of Knowledge of Good and Evil. We threw away that relationship. Mankind started to create his own morality system ever since. And guess what? Lying then entered the world. Hatred entered the world. Murder entered the world. Disease entered the world. Hunger entered the world. Decay and old age entered the world. Death entered the world. The foundation started to change. Fast forward to after the Exodus, mankind was then given a written moral code, now etched in stone, to show what he has been doing wrong all these years, to try and re-establish the foundation. Today the world is not judged by this code unless you still decide to live under that moral code. Jesus came and fulfilled the Law. The Law today is not etched in stone. They are supposed to be etched in your heart. In other words, this Law is supposed to be part of who we are. Is murder wrong? Yes. But Jesus said:

Matthew 5:21-22, (NKJV)

"You have heard that it was said to those of old, 'You shall not murder, and whoever murders will be in danger of the judgment.' But I say to you that whoever is angry with his brother without a cause shall be in danger of the judgment."

The act of murder is wrong by the Law of Moses, but murder is also wrong in your heart, by the new Law of Christ. Burning with hatred inside is wrong. This is why racism is wrong. Just because you have never hurt or killed a person of a different race doesn't mean you are innocent of murder. Your words and hatred of another race are just as bad. It is the same with adultery. The Law says you should not do it. But Jesus said even if you lust in your heart, it is the same thing. This is why we are all guilty of something. If we do these things in our hearts, then it doesn't even matter what our actions actually are. This is another stumbling block for atheists. They always say they don't need a savior because they are good people. They have never murdered and they do not hate. I would actually agree with that statement. Most atheists are good people in a worldly manner. They are morally upright people, based on actions and laws of society, even based on most of the Ten Commandments. But they are not innocent in their hearts. No one is. All fall short of the glory of God (Romans 3:23). This is why we all needed Jesus. His grace now covers us because we cannot be made perfect by our actions. The Law is perfect, but it doesn't make us perfect. Even after trying to follow the Law there still had to be a high priest making atonement. Jesus is now our high priest. The Law was a foundation from God. The Law, though, is now written in your heart and is still from God. Morality has never changed. And if it has never changed, then it cannot be subjective. The foundation is still God. God set up the structure with the family as the next stronghold.

3

The Family Is
The Strongest Bond

RELATIONSHIPS

I was pretty good at baseball, if I do say so myself. My local
all-star team made it to the state finals when I was 15. The state
tournament was held in a small city 150 miles away from my
hometown. It was a three-day tournament. To accommodate all
the families going to the tournament, local families were asked to
host players in their homes. I was lucky to spend time with a neat
family. But when we lost in the tournament and it was time to go
home, I had to say goodbye to the host. I wanted to stay one more
night, but my parents did not want me to do that. I was upset
because I wasn't allowed to stay with the host one more night and
said, "But, Dad, they're family." He looked at me and said with the
most disappointing voice I have ever heard him use, "No, they're
not." I was upset that whole night, but I never really thought about
what I said, and how much it was wrong to say, until later in life.
He was right. They were not family. I had no connections, no

bond with them, except for them being a host for three days. They wouldn't love me like my mom and dad. They wouldn't die for me like my mom and dad. They may not have even cared anything about me if it came down to it. Family is stronger than what I said it was that day. And to this day I am ashamed I said it.

There are plenty of good quotes about family. Michael J. Fox, actor in the movie, *Back to the Future* and television show *Family Ties* said, "Family is not an important thing. It's everything." Family is everything because it was what God based our whole society upon. He is the foundation but the family is the next level. In this chapter, we will look at the family and how it is the strongest bond we have.

God is the strongest piece of the whole structure and is the foundation. If God is the foundation, then things are built on Him. Hebrews 3:4 says it the best:

> *"For every house is built by someone, but God is the builder of everything."*

God built the whole universe. He built this world and this structure with Him as the foundation. He would now build upon Himself with His creation. On the seventh day, He created His most prized creation; the human. As stated in the previous chapter, we are from Him and He wanted to be part of us. After God created the universe and all that it entails, His next step was to establish all relationships. Since we are His greatest creation, the relationship that He wanted the most was one with us.

Our first relationship is and always was supposed to be with Him. He created one human, and that human had a special bond with Him that none of the rest of creation had. We had been given

God's spirit. Man was able to connect with God more than any other part of creation. God walked in the Garden where Adam was placed. God spoke to Adam personally. Some theories even have Adam living alone for millions of years with Him, even before Eve was created. I like the theory because it would connect science and some Biblical gaps. It says Adam lived 930 years, but that was after the "Fall." What about before the "Fall?" How many earth years did Adam live? No one knows. But Genesis 2:16-17 does give us a clue about this topic.

Genesis 2:16-17, (NASB)

"The Lord God commanded the man, saying, 'From any tree of the garden you may eat freely; but from the tree of the knowledge of good and evil you shall not eat, for in the day that you eat from it you will surely die.'"

If Adam didn't start to age or grow old until after he ate from the Tree, then he *could have* lived millions of years. He was able to die after he ate, but the Bible doesn't really say how long it was between Creation and the Fall. It would coincide with science a little more at that point. It would also have given him time to name all of the animals (Gen 2:20) and shut some atheists up about the paradox they claim it is. It isn't one but they claim it is. In any case, it was God and Adam for a while. This is why it is so hard to understand how Adam fell away so easily. If he had this special relationship with God, then how could one fruit and another person who looked good to him, tempt him that much? The first relationship we should have is one with God, not with nature or anything else.

But God gave us even more than just a relationship with Him, even though that should be good enough. He gave us a relationship with others to share, and experience this life with; someone who is like we are. The second relationship He created was a partnership. He created a special relationship that allowed us to be able to share with someone those special times in our lives. He created a husband and wife. Unlike what the theory of evolution states, and even theistic evolution (the idea that God used evolution as part of the creation process) states, there were not millions of people who developed all over the world from different species, or who were created all at once in the beginning. There was one man and one woman, and a bond between them. Now as stated, they may have been in the Garden of Eden for millions of years and never started to age until they ate from the Tree of Knowledge of Good and Evil. Afterward, they were placed under the curse, but nevertheless, they were alone as a species, and also alone with God. God gave them to each other.

Genesis 2:23-24, (NLT)

"At last!" the man exclaimed. "This one is bone from my bone and flesh from my flesh! She will be called 'woman,' because she was taken from 'man.'"

He said: "They will become one." He did not give Adam another man. He did not give Adam another god. He did not give Adam a desire for anything else. He gave Adam and Eve. And to Eve, He gave Adam. The two were supposed to have a one-on-one relationship and procreate. Otherwise, how would they leave their mother and father as we have read about earlier? They were given a gift to share with each other. Before there is a family, there is a bond between man and woman. This is a problem that we have in today's time. We see it as though a family can be at any time, in any way, in any place, and now has many different meanings. You will see this later on. Have I broken that promise yet? Marriage is defined by God, not by us.

The third relationship He created was the family. Adam and Eve had children after their relationship was sealed and from there on, we read about all the children of Adam and Eve, and history was written. Once the family was established, we have the second foundation of the structure of mankind. They were to multiply and fill the earth. They were to have children. After this relationship was created there were no other relationships mentioned until there were communities and civilizations because those relationships are very different. Family is built upon God, the true foundation. A family is defined by God, not by us.

THE POWER OF FAMILY

Family is the strongest bond that we have as humans. It is where we started in life and many times it is all we have at the end of our lives. As the saying goes, friends come and go but family is forever. Or, you can pick your friends but you're stuck with your relatives. Both are accurate and valid. One of the reasons why the family is the strongest bond is because of love. Love is not just an action. Love is not just an emotion. Love is something that, in all actuality, cannot be explained with total accuracy. It is within all of us to be given and to give. We desire it automatically. We want someone to fill the void if we don't have it from others. This love is supposed to be the strongest connection we have in life. As another saying goes, there is nothing like a mother's love. They say that the bond between the newborn and its mother is highly powerful, and may even serve more purposes than just the bonding. I read a very interesting online article from parenting.com called *The New Science of Mother-Baby Bonding*. It said, "A close attachment can prevent diseases, boost immunity, and enhance IQ in your baby" (Deepak Chopra, M.D., 2022). He goes on to say, "Those hugs and kisses are a force of nature more powerful than ever thought. Mother-child bonding has evolved to become a complex physiological process that enlists not just our hearts, but our brains, hormones, nerves, and almost every part of our bodies." There is something about that love. The love is also supposed to be shared by the father, although many probably say they have felt less from them. But ask a child who is hurting what they think is the main cause of their issues. As a teacher, one thing I kept seeing in a student who was depressed or just not happy in class, was that the child never felt the love and support at home, especially from the father. They miss that love. The love from a parent is the most natural love we have, yet many do not have it, and that destroys a child. The reason why a child hurts so much when he or she does not get this love is that inside we know this love is natural. The benefit a child has when the mother is able to bond with her child is beyond important. There is this thing called Mother-Child Bonding that starts in the womb. Linda Palmer, who has an undergraduate degree from the University of Illinois in chemistry with a minor in biology, a Bachelor of Science in human biology, and a Doctorate in Chiropractic Medicine from the National College of Chiropractic said: "When the baby travels through the birth canal, oxytocin -- often called the bonding or love hormone -- is heightened for both the mother and baby." (Linda Palmer, 2014) Fathers can have this attachment too but it takes more physical contact. Richard Fletcher of the University of Newcastle says fathers need eye-to-eye contact and take on some of the duties. The way the father interacts can help with the structure of the brain. (Richard Fletcher, 2014) In both situations, there is a chemical called oxytocin that is released and this bonding is created. The child who had these issues in class would come to me and say, "I don't get why my father doesn't love me." "Isn't he supposed to love me as soon as I was born?" "Aren't your parents supposed to love you?" Too many times they did not get that love and they knew it was supposed to be there. This is not a learned love but it sure can be unlearned. This love is part of the structure of the family. But why is this love not there? I cannot say this for everyone since all are different, but many times it is because the child in today's time is born out of wedlock or in marriages that do not have a whole lot to stand on. I keep seeing things like "My boyfriend and I are expecting our third child." Are you serious? You already have a third child and you're still not married? Or we have the reverse Brady Bunch Syndrome (I think I just made that up). People divorce and marry other people and then *leave* their children from the first marriage behind.

Figure 5
Survey Question About Biological Parents

Question: Your biological parents are:	
Answer	Percentage
Happily married	28%
Divorced	25%
Married, but not happy	23%
Never got married	22%
Widowed	2%
I don't know. I am adopted.	<1%

Source: Personal survey, averages are of freshman students from 2010-2022

When I teach history, I like to actually finish up with modern-day/current events. The last lesson of the year, I always try to teach about their lives, but I use their words. I give them a survey that is very personal. On the survey, one of the questions I ask is, "Are your biological parents..." and then I gave them a few choices (Figure 5). The top three responses were: "happily married," "married but not happy," and "divorced."

When I first did the survey, about ten years ago, the numbers looked different. Divorce and being happily married were always above the others. But the one that is rising among the last of the Millennials and the beginning of the newest Generation Z, is parents "never got married." How can a child feel loved when three of the top four marriage/parental relationships are negative?

The family is supposed to be the main unit that shows love. The numbers from the survey keep telling me that 72% of the students are coming from some household where love is foreign, or not as high as it should be. People decide today to have all kinds of relationships besides actual marriage. And when they do get married, they are choosing to do it in non-traditional ways. Now, a marriage is a marriage. And what I mean by that is, that it really doesn't have to take place in a church or even with some form of clergy performing the ceremony. It's still important and should be taken seriously. If you commit, then you make a commitment. Most of the time, we have these things like being married in a church due to tradition, state legal matters such as status on taxes, or to ease some minds with the sacred ceremony. However, on the other hand, marriage should not be taken lightly. It is sacred in its concept. It also should not consist of anything besides a man and a woman. I know that will make many people, right here and now, angry. I could write at least a whole other chapter on that topic alone, but once again that is a different book. If the law says it is legal in any other way the law is inappropriately written, but I feel it still should be respected. Anyway, there is a major drive by modern society to get rid of traditional marriage ceremonies. Yes, marriage is under fire. Look at Hollywood. Weddings are hardly ever done in churches anymore on television or in movies unless it is some kind of Christmas special on the Hallmark Channel. No clergy is ever invited to perform the wedding. Usually, now, the ceremony is performed by either some Justice of the Peace or a friend who was "ordained" on the Internet. And when the vows are said, they are never done in any traditional way. They don't make actual promises of commitment or make any actual vows. The vows are always written by the two who are getting married and they are only about how they met or how they make each other feel. In other words, they may have built a friendship but they have not found the true love they need for a marriage. I have heard the average Hollywood marriage lasts about 6 years. Is that art imitating life or is it life imitating art? Loving someone's eyes is not a promise to look into their eyes only. Making someone laugh is not a promise to stay faithful. No one promises to stay with anyone through the hard times of life anymore. And there will be hard times. Promises have been taken out of marriage. Sacredness has been taken out of marriage. God has been taken out of the marriage ceremony. God has been taken out of the marriage. God has been taken out of love. All of this means the love of a family is not starting in the right place. It has no real foundation. Without this love, people search for it in other places and those places are not the same in any way, shape, or form. They go to bars. If you meet someone drunk, then you need to stay drunk to keep liking them. They go to clubs. If you meet someone while having fun, then you need to keep having fun to like them. They go to the internet. Guess where they will have to go to keep liking them. I am not saying these marriages cannot work out, but look deep inside, and think about where you met the one you are with, and see if it has a foundation. When people find this alternative to the foundation, they feel like they have found something, but it ends up leaving them still with a hole in their life. Marriage should be seen as the gateway to starting a family. The family is the strongest bond.

Another major family contribution is teaching. Your first lessons in life should be from your family, i.e., your mother and father. No one should have to learn things from the streets. The parents should be the ones who raise the children. It is their responsibility. Even the grandparents should not be the ones to do that. Grandparents should stay out of it as much as possible unless the children are being hurt or the parents are not around. Parents should be ready to raise their own children and have enough knowledge of life to pass it on, or at the least try to do it. The family is where we should first learn about right and wrong. The family should be where our education begins. It is where we should learn about how to live in society, and how to act in public. Whether you agree or not there are right ways to act in public. No one should walk down the street giving obscene signs to everyone. No one should go to a restaurant, and yell at every table while people are trying to have a nice quiet dinner. The family should teach how to honor elders and the past. Whether you don't like the older people or not, they deserve some kind of respect for all they have gone through in life. Families should teach respect for the country and for those in authority. They should teach responsibility. There is more to life than just ourselves. We have a responsibility to others, to the world, and to the environment. And most of all, families should teach to have compassion and mercy for those who need it.

Not only do families teach about the issues already mentioned, they should teach other things such as skills in life, and prepare them for a possible career. They deal with lessons in life, and how to get through times and situations. Many learn career skills as well from the family. Traditional families of old used to pass down survival skills to their children. They learned how to hunt, fish, grow crops, and home economics. Fathers used to pass on building skills and maintenance. Mothers used to pass on cooking and nurturing skills. And there is nothing wrong with the father and mother switching those roles. My point is life skills were taught at home. Today we have children learning all they know in school or on the streets. Neither of those is fit to teach those skills, nor is it their right nor responsibility. There are many family businesses where the affairs are turned over to the children when it is time. There are many generational occupations, such as teachers' children often becoming teachers themselves. Doctors' children become doctors. Police officers' children become police officers and so on. Learning these skills is usually taught early on, and if the child becomes accustomed to the career and likes it, they tend to stay within the family tradition. I learned how to fish from my grandfather. I learned how to drive a car from my father. I learned Judo and wrestling from my father. I learned how to be competitive and to cheat at games from my mother. That is a family joke. But the point remains. I learned most of my life skills from the traditions, practices, and knowledge of my family. And if we did not learn it early on, we tended to learn things from each other later with time. But the most important thing they taught me was that there is a

God and Jesus is my savior. Nothing could compare to that lesson and for that, I am most grateful.

Families also share with each other. There are things you can never share with anyone for they are your deepest and most personal thoughts. And then there are some things you can share with perfect strangers because those things are not that big of a deal. However, this is where the problems of social media come in and the stupidity of many people starts to show. They feel they can and should post anything and everything about their personal lives. They do it to get the attention they feel they deserve or desire. And then they wonder why their lives are miserable, or why they have people who make negative comments on their media pages. Listen, there are things you just do not post and show the world, no matter what. Do you hear that? No matter what! Social media, even with all of its advantages, luxury, and fun has been used as a destructive weapon by those in our society who do not have any values. At school, most of the drama that we have to deal with is that which is started on social media. Why schools have to deal with this is beyond me. There are things you only share with friends and or co- workers because you know they understand you or the situation. They may know your history. They know your patterns in life. They may have even gone through the same thing since you share common characteristics anyway. That is why you probably became their friend in the first place. They may know what makes you cry and what makes you laugh. One of those special friends may even end up being the person you share everything with in life but until then, you still keep things from them for it is not their business. There are things you only share with your family. Your hopes and dreams, your childhood pain, your trials and tribulations in life, and the pain of death; all of these are things that only family members can comfort. Yes, there will be friends as close as a family member, but those are rare. And then there are the things that you share only with the person you picked as the one you promise to share your life with. The family is the strongest bond. But the family is under attack.

SOCIOLOGICAL CHALLENGES TO THE FAMILY

Unfortunately, in today's times we have seen the family break apart, and most of the family values we used to know have gone out the window. Times probably started to change around 1965 when Baby Boomers started to have children called Generation X. Baby Boomers never taught respect for authority, since they were angry with the Vietnam era and the leaders of the time. Generation X never taught honor to their children called Millennials, since Gen X was angry at their parents for the things they did, and they couldn't understand honor. Millennials don't know about responsibility since they became lost in video games and an escape-minded virtual world. They had nothing to pass on to this last generation which is called Generation Z. Generation Z is technically growing up with nothing to learn since all has been given to them already. Baby Boomers started the divorce rates to skyrocket. Generation X never bothered getting married. Millennials have all kinds of relationships and marriage now has a different meaning to them. Again, Generation Z has been abandoned. They do not even understand the concept of a real family. Being a single parent is very common now. When I have parent- teacher conferences the "parent" could be anyone. Often, it is not even the actual parent that shows up, but rather the aunt/uncle or the grandparent. I even had a few "friends of the family" come in to be the representative, because that is all the child had in their life. I will explain later what the generations are composed of and how they respond to this life. Families should be the strongest bond but the family has lost its importance.

One of the classes I had to "pass," to achieve a social studies teacher certification, was sociology. It was a very interesting class. This is the class that probably sent me down the path to studying the differences between the generations. In this class, the main topic was the way society looked at "norms," expectations of people in situations. We have five ways of looking at norms. There are morals, values, mores, folkways, and taboos. What I have noticed is that each generation views these norms differently, hence that makes us a new generation. We will see what that has done to us a little later.

We all have morals. Morals tell us exactly what right and wrong are. But morals need to be defined. These definitions come from what we value. And those values differ from person to person. And because they differ, we start to disagree on what morality is. Then there are "mores." Mores are what we consider normal activity at the time. Mores help us create laws. Even though we have differences of opinion, can we compromise on what should be legal or not? This is why laws change so much. Because what is considered normal, may change within each generation. Smaller local communities will not have the same laws as larger communities. This is where folkways come in. Folkways are local customs versus what others may think. People who live in the mountains are going to have different folkways than those living on a beach. They just act differently. And then there is taboo; something that we all probably have an issue with. Given a topic, something that is not only illegal but also whether it should ever be accepted or not. Taboos are usually accepted by the whole society as being wrong, but those have changed as well over the years. Take a look at Figure 6, for further examples of these different views of life.

Figure 6
Societal Norms of Murder (Using abortion as an example)

Type of Norm:	Concept:	Example:
Moral, one system	Right vs Wrong	Do not murder or take any life
Value, depends on person	Person vs person	Abortion is murder, Abortion is not murder
More, depends on the law	Legal vs illegal	Abortion is legal but challenged
Folkway, depends on locality	Custom vs Society	Those states with stronger religious backgrounds may limit abortions
Taboo, one system	Accepted vs unaccepted	Back-alleys abortions happen

Source: Examples are mine. Categories are typically accepted terms of sociology.
They are not necessarily hierarchical.

Family teaches values. Values make us who we are. Values are different from morals. Values are the things that we hold dear. Values are divided by cultures into mores, folkways, and taboos. Families do not teach morals. God laid down the morals at Creation. Morals are not learned behavior. They are common sense and should be inherited by us. There is only one right way on some topics, the rest are wrong. They are NOT subjective. Morals cannot be changed, but they are challenged by some people. The challenge would be unfortunate and wrong, but nevertheless real, as we will see. In reality, all values, mores, and folkways should be the same. They should be the same as our morals but humanism divides them and adds separation. From there, we get groups within our culture. That is the next chapter. All of these should be based on the morals of God.

Morals are the standards we live by. Morals tell us what is *universally* right and wrong. These are locked in. They do not change. There are absolutes in this world. There is right and wrong in this world. Morals define that for us. And again, these were given by God. Values come out of these morals. Those hopes and dreams mentioned earlier stem from our values. They define how deep our morals are. These values should be based on the moral standards of God. Such as murder, the taking of a life, and being wrong is amoral. A value would be defining what murder actually is. People, unfortunately, will have different ideas of what murder is, and that is where our personal values come in. Someone may value the life of a baby, and think it is immoral to take away that life, such as with abortion, and would consider it murder. Others will not have that value about abortion but still consider the act of murder to be immoral. They just don't think abortion fits that definition of murder.

Why would the act of murder be wrong anyway? Humanism of course would say it is common sense. I would agree. But why would it be common sense? They say it is common sense because humans came to realize over time that it was wrong. This is why atheists say they do not need to know God in order to know that murder is wrong; a very true argument I had with another atheist. No. It is common sense because it was put inside us. We started to know the difference when

Adam ate from the Tree of Knowledge of Good and Evil. It has been common sense ever since.

God did not want death. Mankind (Adam) chose to die when he disobeyed Him. And then in the second generation of the human race, we have murder (Cain killed Abel). Mankind now chooses to murder. Cain pretty much became antisocial. "Antisocial personality disorder, sometimes called sociopathy, is a mental condition in which a person consistently shows no regard for right and wrong and ignores the rights and feelings of others." (See resource page). Cain showed that about himself when God asked him where Abel was after he murdered him. Watch how Cain responded to the murder he committed.

Genesis 4:9 (ESV).

*"Then the LORD said to Cain, "Where is Abel your brother?" He said, "I do not know; **am I my brother's keeper?**"*

Cain had no regard for his brother anymore, or his own actions. He did not see the wrong he did. He only tried to deflect the problem and cover up what he did. Cain did not have the moral standard that he should have had, and so he did not value life the way he should have. However, he valued his own life later when God sent him away.

Genesis 4:13-14 ISV

"My punishment is too great to bear," Cain told the Lord. "You're driving me from the soil today. I'll be hidden from you, and I'll wander throughout the earth as a fugitive. In the future, whoever finds me will kill me."

He sure cared about murder then, didn't he? Sociopaths, such as Charles Manson or even Cain, may have had values but they did not have moral standards. If his values were based on Godly morals, he would not have murdered so easily. If family values are based on God, then the family structure has a good foundation. If these values are not based on God, then values are based on lesser things, like mankind and its culture. And that is not a good thing.

Family teaches values. Values should be the same as morals which were based on the foundation of God. A family should be based on God.

The family is the strongest bond. The culture definitely is not.

4
It Doesn't Take a Village

Have you ever wondered how cultures got started? This is a topic I would love to have more time to study. I would love to see how each culture developed, where they came from, and how they influenced other cultures. I first got the desire to learn more about this topic, when I took an anthropology class in college. It was one of those classes required to become a social studies teacher, which I mentioned earlier. Anthropology is a fascinating social science. I would also like to see how each community in these cultures developed differently from others over time. Isn't it neat to see how the accents in Boston are very much different from those in Chicago? What happened that made those changes? Did the accent change the way the community is? Did the accent play a major factor in how that region developed? It sounds almost impossible, but I would almost guarantee that the accent changed the area, and not just the area changing the accent. Culture has become the driving force in our country. In this chapter, we will look at how our culture started to take over, break down, and destroy the true foundation.

Over the last few decades, thanks to former First Lady and former Senator Hillary Clinton, there has been a saying that it takes a village to raise a child. You hear it everywhere. That saying is a lie. Or at the least, it is a statement of ignorance. This statement alone takes away the importance of a family. It definitely takes away the foundation of God, because it places importance on humanity. That is called humanism. Once the family has a breakdown, or the family is not built upon the foundation of God, people start to look for other foundations. Cultures, as a whole, started to become more important.

Anyway, to live in a certain community and to feel like you belong to that community, you will have to learn the customs of the community. Cultures developed out of the traditions and customs of communities. Learning the language is the first key. Without communication, you are living lost. Learning the laws is the second key. Knowing the laws of a community keeps you from upsetting the locals, even if the laws are stupid. But to be accepted completely into a community or a culture, you also need to know what is expected of you. Learning the values, mores, folkways, and taboos of a community will help you live more comfortably in a community, although you do not have to agree with the citizens there. You need to learn the history of the region. You need to understand the common ways of life. Cultures develop over generations of time and they created the societal norms that were discussed earlier. Cultures should be based on families that are based on God. But cultures today are based on the ideology of humanism as their foundation. The norms and expectations have changed. But what has each generation done to change those norms? How has the culture of each generation destroyed the original foundation?

THE GENERATIONS

As of the year 2022 AD, in the United States, we have about 5 established and active generations. The generations are the Silent Generation, the Baby Boomers, Generation X, Millennials (Generation Y), and Generation Z. For those who know me, this is one of the favorite subjects I like to teach. I have looked at the generations, and have studied them to see the differences. As a history teacher/historian, I wanted to see how different we are, and how we have been affected by each generation. It helped me understand my students better, as well. This will just be the short version, but I think to understand how our culture has diminished the foundation of God, it is needed.

Figure 7
Generations of the United States

Generation	Howe and Strauss	Population Reference Bureau	Center for Generational Kinetics	Tim Herzog
Silent Generation	1925-1945	1928-1945	Before 1945	1925-1945
Baby Boomers	1946-1964	1946-1964	1946-1964	1945-1965
Generation X	1965-1979	1965-1980	1965-1976	1965-1985
Gen Y Millennials	1980-2000	1981-1996	1977-1995	1985-2005
Generation Z	2000-now	1997-2012	1996-now	2005-now

Source: Rosenberg, Matt. "Generational Names in the United States." ThoughtCo, Feb. 12, 2020, thoughtco.com/names-of-generations- 1435472., except for the last column

Depending upon whom you ask there will be differing opinions about when these generations start and stop. You can see a few examples in Figure 7. Although they all agree on the names of the generations, an economist would have a different definition than say a historian would. The historian would have a different definition than someone in the business world, and so forth. The business world seems to shrink each generation as we go. Such as they have the Baby Boomers ranging about 20 years in total. They have Generation X being 17 years. They have Millennials existing for 15 years. They have Generation Z existing for only 10 years. They already have labeled the 5-year-olds as Generation Alpha. This is because the business world is trying to develop technology to push the future, so they can get rich. They want to drive the economy and create the gadgets that each generation would want. There are many definitions for the word generation, but the best one is this from Merriam-Webster.com, the third entry, "the average span of time between the birth of parents and that of their offspring." How can a generation then be only 15 years old on average? It can't be in most terms. The Center for Generational Kinetics is way off.

However, generations are hard to define perfectly. There are gaps and overlapping. The gaps between the generations, from anyone's standpoint, will have some overlapping, or a margin of error, if you will, by perhaps 2-3 years. You could be a certain age yet act like someone in a connected generation, depending upon what you value and how you are raised. Generations are defined by the events of their lifetime and their reactions.

Each generation gives birth, in most scenarios, to the next generation, as Merriam-Webster states. Some exceptions would be those who were older when they had children, or (those who have had many children) and might have two or more children ending up being in two different generations. A good example of this exception was my mother-in-law. She was from the Silent Generation. Her children should be Baby Boomers, but one is actually young enough to be in Generation X. My mother-in-law happened to be born closer to the end of her generation, and if both of her children were born closer together when she was really young, they both would have been Baby Boomers. But she had one child when she was 25 and she had the other child when she was 30. The 5-year difference between the girls, in this case, was actually enough of a gap that they are considered two different generations. As a result, her two girls act differently sometimes and have different values every now and then. There is usually a parent-child generation gap that causes the parent and child to argue a lot. A generation gap is when there is a difference of opinion between two consecutive generations, usually based on the changing values of the times. This scenario is not the case with the younger daughter. My wife and her mother were actually two generations apart, not just one. They were very close like a grandchild would be with a grandparent. I don't think they had ever disagreed with each other. Sometimes I think they shared the same brain. But in contrast, my parents were born at the beginning of the Baby Boomers. I was born in the very next generation (X). We are close but we are nothing like my wife and her mom. Hence our generation gap happened a lot more. The other exception would be for those who were very young when they had children. Many times, the parent and child are within the same generation. A fifteen-year-old has a child. There isn't enough of a gap between them at times. These are the parents who are more friends *with* their children, instead of actual parents *to* their children. They party with them and do other activities with them, besides teaching them. But the main issue is, the child doesn't have a parent that acts as a parent. There develops a case of jealousy between them, as an older brother or sister would be. So, what are the generations and what are they like?

THE SILENT GENERATION

Those in the Silent Generation were born between 1925 and 1945. There were about 50 million born in that generation. They could be called Traditionalists, the GI Generation, and the Depression Era children. This generation started a little after World War One ended, and it stopped when World War Two ended. This generation has seen the most deaths than any other generation. They knew their parents fought in the First World War only to end up fighting the second one on their own. They were born during the Spanish Flu Pandemic which killed 675,000 Americans, more than both world wars combined. They grew up during the Great Depression. They saw things many of us praying to God will never have to see. They were the first to see modern automation and electronics as technology. They saw radios, television, and cars develop. They built our highways. They lived a simple life. They are storytellers, and they have many stories to tell. They want people to hear their wisdom. They will most certainly tell you about life. They built the American dream on tradition and built the American value system. They taught us to respect, and how to get through life's struggles. Families still stayed together. Children were not left alone if it could be helped. People looked for work and were expected to honor those who did.

They kept us going. They know how to survive. They were far from perfect, however. Unfortunately for this generation, the reason why they are called the Silent Generation is that they remained silent about important cultural topics. Family secrets were kept in the family. Children were seen but not heard, and sometimes abused without any definition to label it. Abuse and neglect were family issues only. Women were kept at home. Some topics at the dinner table were not appropriate---taboo. Unfortunately, racism was an accepted part of life, and many are still in that mindset. Again, they were far from perfect but they had one major thing that would define them. They had God as their foundation. They held onto values that were still close to Godly morals, with some exceptions. Even with all the things wrong at the time, they held onto hope and God. And with that foundation, they knew how to survive. But times were ready to change. The Silent Generation remained too silent and let the next generation change too many things, including the foundation.

THE BABY BOOMERS

Those in the Baby Boomer Generation were born in the range 1945-1965. There were about 75 million born in that generation. Up until then, that was the largest ever in the history of the United States. The gap was 25 million more being born between them and their parents. They are also known as the Hippie Generation in the first half and then the Yuppie Generation in the second half. They were the Flower Children and the Me Generation. The last two really explain it all; drugs and selfishness. This generation started when World War Two ended. It was started because the largest fighting force of all time in our country came home from war. They had spent months perhaps years away from their significant other, and you can imagine the rest of what happened next.

They grew up during the Korean War, and many fought in the Vietnam War; the event that will end their generation. They grew up during the beginning of the Cold War and felt the dangers rise as the years went by. Tensions came to a boiling point for them as a child, due to the Cuban Missile Crisis. They grew up tired of what they saw. They wanted change. These are your first major liberals in the United States. Humanism was launched full-scaled. The changes they made, seemed like they were the right things. They fought for civil rights, personal freedoms, and the environment. They protested traditional culture and became what is known as the counterculture. The VCR, microwave, and jet engines were the new technology of their time. They taught us freedom of individual matters. They taught us that individuality is important. And perhaps their biggest contribution was their fight for civil rights. But with all of the things they did that may have seemed right, they made some changes that destroyed the culture, the family, and our foundation. Prayers were removed from school in 1962. They started the drug culture. During the 1960s and 1970s as the Baby Boomers started to come of age, the culture had become drug-infested. Woodstock would become the poster child of the Baby Boomers. David F. Musto, M.D. from the University of Washington School of Medicine, was the leading expert on drug usage in the 1970s said, "During the 1960s, the entrenched commitment to law enforcement confronted an unprecedented rise in the nature and extent of illicit drug use. The transformation, especially in marijuana use, was associated with social and political turmoil, including the deep fissures caused by the Vietnam War, the civil rights movement, and profound demographic changes as the "Baby Boom" generation approached maturity." (David F. Musto, 1996). Songs were filled with drug innuendos, such as the Beatles' "Lucy in The Sky with Diamonds," meaning LSD. Marijuana took over and started to lead to other drugs. We have been addicted ever since. When the Boomers grew up, they broke apart the family unit. See, when they were young and high, they "fell in love" but when they had to finally come back to reality and find careers, they had to come down off drugs and look at the one they chose. They realized they didn't really love the person they chose and the divorce rates skyrocketed in the 1980s. Rates went from 9.2% in 1960 up to 22.6% in 1980. (Bowling Green State University, 2022)

Baby Boomers chose to have a culture of free love, and when they became older, sexually transmitted diseases skyrocketed, as well and we saw the emergence of AIDS. They were rebellious in their optimism and are now blind to the division they caused. The protests became riots. Birmingham, New York City, Detroit, Los Angeles, Chicago, and Kent State University saw some of the worst riots and murders in our lifetime. Division across the United States became apparent and would lead to the separation we have today. In the year 1993, things really changed. The Baby Boomers became the leaders of the country. Even Northern Illinois University claims the year 1993, as what they called the "Year of the Baby Boomer" (See resource page). They had risen to the top of the workforce. They had become collegiate educators pushing liberal and humanistic ideologies. We had our first Baby Boomer elected as president, Bill Clinton. They were in charge for the next 24 years (Clinton, Bush, Obama). They drove wedges into society. Instead of using national tragedies to unite Americans, they used them for their own political gain, especially Presidents Clinton and Obama. By 2016, we had become so divided due to Baby Boomer politics, that we decided to elect two more from the Silent Generation (Trump, Biden). Unfortunately, the last two haven't been so silent. Thomas Carothers, Senior Vice President for studies at the Carnegie Endowment for International Peace, and director of Carnegie's Democracy, Conflict, and Governance Program said that right now a "powerful alignment of ideology, race, and religion renders America's divisions unusually encompassing and profound. It is hard to find another example of polarization in the world," (Pew Research, 2020). I am not saying that things were going great before this. Civil rights were needed. There needed to be changes. But there are right ways and wrong ways to accomplish things. As this book was being written in 2020, we witnessed riots going on in Seattle, Chicago, New York City, and other places. People protested violence, yet more people were being killed during the riots than the number of people being killed they were protesting for. People feel the louder and more dramatic you are, the more people will hear you, and that is not accurate. Causing division is not a solution. Following humanistic values is not a solution. The foundation of God is gone. The family is being destroyed and now due to the Baby Boomers, the culture has been corrupted leaving the next generation full of anger.

GENERATION X

Those in Generation X were born in the range of 1965-1985. The Center for Generational Kinetics says this generation only lasted eleven years (Figure 7). See how they are wrong? There were about 70 million born in that generation. They are known as the

Lost Generation, and that is one true statement. Apparently, the Center thinks so too, since they only consider it to be eleven years' worth. Many times, this generation is overlooked. They get lost in between the Baby Boomers and the Millennials. Look at politics. You have Baby Boomers leading the country and companies and the Millennials making their voices heard (too loudly sometimes, like a certain young Congressperson from New York's 14th Congressional District as of 2022). Gen Xers are also known as the Latch Key kids and the MTV Generation. They grew up letting themselves into their homes after school, and then they weren't being watched once they were inside because both of their Baby Boomer parents went to work. They let the family traditions go to waste. Dave Roos, a freelance writer said in 2017, "Although the term "latchkey kid" first appeared in the 1940s to describe young children taking care of themselves after school while dad fought in the war and mom went off to work, the anxiety over latchkey kids really exploded in the United States in the late 1970s and early 1980s. Higher divorce rates and more job opportunities for women left a reported three million 6 to 13-year-old children fending for themselves after school in 1982." (Dave Roos, 2017) Boomers were more worried about their careers, their rights, and themselves than their own children. Dinners were not held at the table anymore, let alone have any conversations at the dinner table. I grew up in a lower-middle-class family, and we eventually got to the middle class. My parents are Baby Boomers. They were not bad parents. They really don't fit their generation's description, but I don't think we had family meals after I turned the age of 15. My mom got a job to help out with finances, and I was old enough to make meals on my own. But now, when I think about it. When did fast-food restaurants really become the most popular? Fast food started around the late 1950s, but the degree of competition didn't hit until the mid-1980s. This was the time when Gen Xers were growing up and needed dinners. Anna Diamond, a reporter for the Smithsonian Magazine said, "Fast food [took off] in large part because of the highway system that we built in the 1950s and the 1960s. America started driving more than ever before, and we rearranged our cities based on car travel, for better or worse. And it was a natural business response to the American on- the-go kind of lifestyle." (Anna Diamond, 2019). I can remember when a certain restaurant that used to post how many people they had served on their signs, had served less than 50 million. If you remember that then you are showing your age. And now they can't even post it anymore because they have served too many, including me still 5-10 times a month. That company stopped keeping records in 1994, if that tells you anything. Fast food was king.

The beginning of the Vietnam War started this generation. The end of the Cold War ended it. The war in Vietnam changed everything in our country. It was a war many did not believe in. Baby Boomers hated it and pretty much vowed to change things because of it. Generation X is a result of those changes and the values that were changed. Gen Xers value individuality because they were left home alone, had no supervision, and had to live on their own. It is what the Boomers left them; be individuals. Again, it was a good idea but it was done wrong. Gen Xers value style and fads to show who they were extenuating their individuality.

They value money because they were the first generation to be worse off than the one before. When the Yuppy half of the boomers grew up and became very selfish by trying to "keep up with the Joneses," they spent a lot of money leaving their children with no "dowries," if you will. In the mid- 1990s, Generation X became the first to have college expectations, and the trend of becoming the first in their families as college graduates, became prominent. (US Census Bureau, Current Population Survey); I am an example of that fact. The computer, the internet, and video games were the new technology. In actuality, they were the first gamers (Atari came out in 1977). This generation was driven by their anger. Movies like *The Breakfast Club* and *Ferris Bueller's Day Off* say it all for Generation X. This is why the sounds of Heavy Metal and "old school" Rap were very successful. Listen to the songs that were fed to them. Words were about getting wild and partying because they wanted to forget the anger or use the anger to live. Songs like Quiet Riot's "Cum on Feel the Noise," and Beastie Boys, "You Gotta Fight for Your Right to Party" are prime examples. Now this is my music, and I still listen to it all, but when I feel like burning off steam, I listen to it even more. I used to sit in my room and listen to my music playing my air guitar and drums all the time. I would make so much noise putting on my own concert upstairs in my room, that my parents probably thought I was crazy, and wondered what I was doing that was so annoyingly loud.

Generation X grew up angry, and it is still inside them. With no supervision, this generation partied way too much, and the drugs escalated into cocaine. It was even the beginning of when the heroin epidemic started. They became selfish, which was learned from their parents. They became pessimistic, which was opposite their parents, on purpose. And because of this selfishness, they decided that they would have relationships, but not take responsibility for them.

Because of this pessimism, divorce started to give way to people not even getting married, since they saw no advantage in it.

Motivation levels started to drop. The culture broke down more, and Generation X lost its foundation and lost hope. It truly became the Lost Generation. They have become X'ed out of life. We wanted to party like it was 1999 because we knew the new millennium was not going to be to our advantage. The new Millennium…how would we raise our children?

MILLENNIALS

Those in the Millennial Generation, sometimes known as Generation Y, were born in the range 1985-2005. There were 95 million born in that generation, the largest ever born in history. They are also known as the We Generation, the Entitlement Generation, and the Gamers. They hate being called the Entitlement Generation but if there was one term that defined them the most, it is that. Most were born during peacetime after the Cold War had ended in 1990 with the fall of the Berlin Wall, the reunification of Germany, and the fall of the Soviet Union. They had not seen the problems of wars like the others before them had seen, nor had known the fear the others had like nuclear war. So, when the tragic events of 9/11 happened, it was new to them. They had never seen the world have issues like the one that day created. They had no idea what tragedy was like in the world. However, they did know what tragedy was like at home. Their parents, who were probably never married or divorced, argued over custody (Figure 5 back in Chapter 3). Fathers weren't around in their lives, and teen moms became more of an accepted norm. They feel that because life gave them these things, and then seeing the terror of 9/11 change the world, that they deserve better and someone needs to give it to them. In reality, of course, they do deserve a better life. But also, in reality, they think things should be given to them and that life screwed them over; like they are the only ones who had bad things happen to them. Their anger did not stay in the homes as Generation X did. They took their anger to the outside world. School shootings became rampant in their generation. From 1970-1990, the time most Generation X was in school, there was an average of 17 shootings per year. But from 1991-2011, the time when most Millennials were in school, there was an average of 30 shootings per year. (CHDS, 2023) They want an easier life and they want things now. They have no patience. Fast food isn't even fast enough for them. Now we have fast food being delivered at home with the onset of personal delivery systems that dash to your door. Fast. Food. Being. Delivered. They value their own desires and don't care what everyone else has done for them, because they "deserve it".

Millennials want to be connected to the world. Social media is the way they communicate. They don't know how to have a normal or rational conversation face-to-face. After all, how much can you say with only 242 characters? Emojis can only go so far. When they do have a conversation, they don't know the difference between whispering and yelling since the internet can't show them that. You can't verbally speak in all CAPS. Cell phones and online gaming were now the new technology and they ate it up and are still eating it. They search for everything online because it has already been done for them. Every conversation with them seems like another opportunity to search the web. They are book- smart, but they are the dumbest when it comes to common sense. My colleague had a student who would not get off his cell phone after he kept telling him to put it away. Finally, after the fourth time the teacher told him to put it away, the student looked at him and said, "If I put it away, then how will I know when someone is texting me?" If you don't get that, you may be a millennial. No common sense. They want to get rich fast without working for it, another entitlement. They are the largest "entrepreneurs" out there. In 2022, 36% of Millennials claim to be entrepreneurs. (Statista Research Department, 2022) In layman's terms--- unemployed, waiting for something to happen to them. I have taught through this whole generation and they just wanted the answers given to them. They would rather "Google" the question than read a full article that has the answer (and something to learn) for them.

Now they have done some good things. They have taught us that all people need to be accepted, notice I said accepted and not tolerated; a different book. They didn't try to do this, but they taught us that people need to be heard, because when they were growing up no one listened to them since their parents weren't there or were too busy arguing. They don't know what real relationships are, since they have no examples to live by. Their grandparents are divorced and their parents are not married (Figure 5). They don't see the need for or have never been taught responsibility, so they don't show it. They don't know how to show respect to others. They do not honor anyone older than them, nor do they honor the experience older people have. They feel their voices are the most important, and they have to get the last word in or they will say "whatever," if they don't agree with any results. January 10, 2019, Joe Liebermann, an older Democratic leader who was Al Gore's VP candidate in the 2000 election, tried to give advice to Alexandria Ocasio-Cortez. Her response was not "thank you," or "Can we talk," or anything that would add to the conversation.

No. Her response was, "Who Dis?" Who dis? Real respectful and grateful to someone who was trying to help.

They can't stand this but they do feel entitled. The world is theirs and they deserve it. But, even with all of the connections to this world that they have, they still feel all alone and isolated. And on top of all of this, the drugs are now fentanyl and meth and getting worse. The culture has now completely broken down. The foundation is all but wiped away. There is no real family value out there. Leaving the last of these generations searching for something, searching for anything, to have hope in.

GENERATION Z

The latest generation is Generation Z. Those in this generation were born in 2005 and are still being born. Right now, there are about 50 million in this generation. They probably have a few years left or so of being born before a new generation starts, so their numbers will probably not be as high as the last three. Personally, it is quite interesting we call them Generation Z, the last letter of the alphabet. Perhaps this is prophetic of what we have become; another book. They are also known as Zoomers for being very much like Boomers in their values. They are known as post- Millennials and the iGeneration. They were born during a historic milestone, the first "black" president being elected in the United States. They were born during the Great Recession. They were born after 9/11, and have no idea what it was about. Terrorism has always been a part of their lives. ISIS and al-Qaeda were now common names and are almost forgotten about. This generation was born in the middle of tragedies and hardships. I have seen a change in the last few years of teaching. I don't think I have flat-out seen the true mentality of Generation Z yet, but the students are starting to change. From what I have seen, they are more motivated than earlier Millennials, so far. They value a new world, perhaps even a new world order where globalization is the new system. They want more economic opportunities. They want jobs! They do not like the systems of the United States like politics, economics, or religious systems, which connects them to Boomers. Virtual life is about all they really know. They go to all the virtual learning sites. Snapchat and TikTok are their hide-outs. They know all about Zoom, Google Hangouts, and other online meeting places for education. Alexa and Siri are their best friends. When I asked them what they "want in life" they answered with "solving social issues," "solving environmental issues," and "discovering and inventing." I fear for them because I have to ask myself, what is their foundation? They are hopeful and energetic, but what do they have to look forward to? Boomers stole their religious rights. Generation X and Millennials destroyed their hope. They are disconnected and all alone even more than Millennials. Do they have structure? Do they have a strong and correct foundation? Or is the culture going to get them? Are we completely broken? Is the foundation completely gone? Can the "village" help?

THE RISE OF THE VILLAGE

When my classes get to the times of nationalism (1848- 1914), we look at how countries either pull themselves together based on the commonality of the people, or how they can be torn apart based on the differences of the people. One of the major themes we look at is language since it is the strongest of all cultural bonds.

Language probably defines culture more than any other factor. Why does language do that? It is probably because families all talk the same, and cultures develop out of families. Languages are grouped by a category called "family".

As families grew and became too big for one household and as people listened to God and heard His words, "*For this reason, a man shall leave his father and his mother, and shall be joined to his wife; and they shall become one flesh.*" (Genesis 2:24, AMP), they left their original homes and their parents and spread throughout the world. Some families stayed within communication distance of others. The rest moved beyond that, but probably kept within some communicating distance of some they knew, all except for Cain that is. They started to settle down. They were no longer just hunters and gatherers. They became agriculturalists. Depending on whom you ask, some say that people started to settle 500,000 years ago. Some say 20,000 years ago, and some say 8,000. Some like Michael Price, a reporter for www.sciencemag.org reported, "Sometime about 10,000 years ago, the earliest farmers put down their roots—literally and figuratively." (Michael Price, 2017). The Bible states it was roughly 6000 years ago and has never wavered. Anyway, one way or another people settled down into communities and developed cultures out of this. Different cultures all over the world developed. Based on the separation of families, all of the races, ethnic groups, nationalities, and what have you, started to develop. Languages solidified. Religious beliefs then separated, along with the spreading of people, and were distorted from the truth. Values changed. Mores, laws, folkways, and taboos now differed from culture to culture. One thing that did not change was the moral standard; only people's interpretations of what morals are.

Once communities developed, and people that were not original family members started to interact, everyday differences of opinions naturally soon came after. When family differences of opinions lead to arguments, most of those are settled by the silent treatment, or just due to time and the fact you have to live under one roof to survive. But differences between non-family members usually cause resentment, and may even lead to things like revenge resulting in murders and long-term conflicts such as the famous one between the Hatfields and the McCoys, and even up to the consequence and the destruction of full-scale war. Yes, that is the extreme but I wanted to prove a point, and we all know this did actually happen.

When people in the communities realized that they could not settle their differences on their own without some sort of violence or escalation, they turned to mediators; hence the creation of government and man's laws. Famous laws were created such as the Ur-Nammu law around 2000 BC in Sumeria and the Code of Hammurabi in Babylon around 1750 BC. The Ten Commandments were around 1500 BC for comparison. The Ur-Nammu law is the oldest known written law. Here is a problem for evolutionists; if modern mankind (homo sapien) is 300,000 years old then how and why did it take 298,000 years to get a written law? The oldest known writing, not written law but just writing, is the Kish Tablet, found in modern-day Iraq, and that was 3500 BC. That I actually believe. If mankind has only been around since let's say 3930 BC (that is my personal calculation) then 400 years of developing writing skills would make more sense than 298,000 years. Anyway, laws were created to govern the disputes between non-family people in society. Families have values. Society though has laws. Villages abuse laws and distort the values. Why would we want the village to raise our children?

VILLAGE LAWS

Now I am not against laws. As for the reasons already mentioned throughout this book, they are most certainly needed, but they have to have some kind of limit. I do not believe in dictatorships. Laws are a form of structure. Laws are for order and they do add to that sense of security, stability, and serenity talked about in Chapter 1. When laws are based on religious practices, then we have what is called a theocracy being established. Most would frown upon that. I would for the most part, since most religions (all but one) are wrong, but I could support a theocracy as long as the laws allowed for interpretation. I do not support a theocracy without any representation or one with abusive laws just for control. Again, that is another book; please do not take that out of context.

Laws help society. Common-sense laws are the best. Such as, we keep using murder as an example, so let's keep using it; murder. It is common sense that murder is wrong. So, why do we have it written down as a law? To make it clear I guess, and so that no one can ever say that they didn't know it was wrong. But this law makes sense. There are other common-sense laws. No stealing. No lying (under oath). No coveting (abuse of neighbor's possessions). All of those are common-sense laws. Laws though, become destructive to society when they become overbearing and outright ridiculous; no longer common sense. According to www.stupidlaws.com in 1987, it was illegal for people in San Francisco to store their own stuff in their own garage. Apparently, only cars are allowed in garages. One has to wonder how this law came into being. Is it common sense to limit your space in your garage to only your car? What happens to the space when you don't have a car in San Francisco? Or can you call the space an "outside closet" so you can get around the law? It is an interesting website to read through. There are so many stupid laws that I couldn't possibly post them all here. The point is there are laws that are just not needed. Society goes hog-wild creating all of these laws thinking they will solve all of the issues but all they usually do is end up causing even more issues such as lawsuits, protests, and addendums to the stupid laws. Too many times laws start to intervene in the personal lives of people. The village that is now proverbially supposed to raise a child, is destroying the child with its intervention. It does not take a village to raise a child. It is neither their right nor their responsibility to raise someone's child.

TOO MANY VILLAGE LAWS

I cannot stand the way culture is in today's time. I know many people think that if you are "woke" and "progressive," then you are advancing and making society better and allowing it to grow. The exact opposite is true. Again, do not take me the wrong way. I am a full believer in individual decision-making, but if your foundation is weak and not on God then it will not matter how "woke" you are or think you are. Freedom is what we were supposed to have. God gave us free will. We are supposed to make decisions. We were supposed to live with God and be free to do all things but one. Don't eat from that tree. We have free will, but there are consequences for doing things that are immoral. Atheists say that if there is some form of punishment, then it is not a choice. Think about it. We could do a million things. We could have chosen to do anything we wanted to. Adam could have walked away from one act. Adam could have performed millions of acts, but he chose to eat from the one tree that was not allowed. Once we ate from that tree we allowed oppression, suppression, and repression to become part of our existence. We became slaves to sin. God wanted us to be free. When He sent Jesus, He freed us from this sin. Anyway, today if we see some kind of issue, one of the first things we feel we need to do is create a law that deals with that topic. Need a STOP sign? Go get a law passed. Need money for a program? Go get a law passed. Need education? Go get a law passed. Need to stop racism? Go get a law passed. Need to protect yourself? Go get a law passed. It seems like every time we turn around, we need a new law to govern us. According to www.govtrack.us as of mid-2020, the 116th Congress (Jan. 2019- Jan. 2021) has passed 142 laws. The 115th Congress (Jan. 2017- Jan. 2019) passed 443. Since 1973 the US Congress has enabled nearly 8000 laws. Think about that. 8000 new laws were passed. Why were so many passed? It was to make sure our culture does what it is supposed to do. But look at the results. Did the laws stop murder? No. Did they stop school shootings? No. Did they stop a person from running the red light? No. All the laws did was to make more things illegal, not fix the issue. Laws originally were only meant to show what is wrong, not used to control people's lives. However, there are certain groups of people that feel differently about that.

The problem with this part of our structure is that we think laws will solve our issues. If we think there is too much killing done by guns, people want gun laws. But the killing will still go on. If not by guns, then knives, swords, axes, bows and arrows, rocks, fists, and any other object someone can get their hands on. I hate guns. I hate what most of them stand for. But if I was a politician, I would never try to take them all away. I believe we should have common-sense laws about them, such as all guns should be registered as soon as they are made, since they can be used for deadly force. People need to take classes before they can get one, since it takes responsibility to use a gun, after all, we do it for cars. No one under the age of 21 should be allowed to register for one since no child should have a need for any. All gun shops need to be monitored, inventoried, and audited. But removing all guns will not help. People will still be violent. Making harsher punishment for using them will not help. People will still respond out of emotions at times, and won't think before they react. No. The problem with guns is not having them, but how they are being used, and why they are being used. Criminals will still get them. The issue is why people feel they *need* them. I would love to live in a world where we feel guns are unnecessary, especially for defending yourself. I want to live in a world where guns are just for sport, in the Olympics.

If we think there are too many abortions, people want abortion laws. But will laws stop abortions? No. People will still get them somehow. I do not like abortions. I feel they are immoral. But again, the issue here is not the fact that we have them, the issue is *why* we have them. People on the "pro-choice" side say they are women's rights. They stress that abortions allow a woman to choose especially if her life or the child's life is in danger, or if there was rape or incest. That is a hard argument to top. But, depending on whom you ask, the percentages of abortions are low for those reasons. I looked at a few sites to gather some information.

Figure 8
Abortion Reasons

	Medical	Rape/ Incest	Age/ Parental control	Economy / No more children	Interfere with life
graphs.net*	12%	1%	N/A	75%	13%
rampages.us	6%	1%	11%	29%	53%
conservapedia.com	7%	0.1%	8%	45%	40%
guttmacher.org**	7%	0.5%	20%	25%	55%
Averages	<10%	<1%	10-15%	40-45%	35-40%

Source: Graphs.net, rampages.us, conservapedia.com, and guttmacher.org, *had to interpret some answers, ** had to combine and interpret some answers

Finding accurate information on this topic was hard to do. Many of the charts cannot be compared equally to each other. Some choices were the "top reason" only. Some choices were the top reasons, but where they could choose more than one answer. Guttmacher Institute seemed to be the most used on websites, as their reference. On average, less than 10% total get abortions due to hard case situations. Less than 15% are done due to age and/ or parental control over the underage child. Less than 45% are done for economic reasons which include having other children, school costs, and family bills. And the rest, about 40% feel a child will interfere with the woman's life somehow or some way beyond the other reasons. I would almost guarantee that most of those are done out of wedlock. Abortion is not the problem. Abortion is a symptom of the bigger problem, the culture, the village that Hillary wants to raise our children. 1% of abortions are caused by the sickness of men. No one should have to live through the atrocities of rape or incest. Very few abortions though, are ever done due to rape or incest. Some abortions are due to, for lack of a better word, selfishness. Stay with me on this. I am not trying to sound heartless. I don't mean to say selfishness as in ego, pompousness, or having a major issue with self-importance. I mean selfishness as in not seeing the big picture. Think about it. What mother would not die for their child? So, getting an abortion due to the mother's health is a selfish reason because there is more to the story. Any good mother, and for that statement any good father, would die for their children. If a mother saw that her child was ready to get hit by a car, would the mother stand there and watch, (claiming her life would have been in danger), or would she dive in front of the vehicle to save her child? She would put her life in danger. I can see though these two reasons for abortions almost as being valid. But let's look at the other reasons. If you don't want any more children due to them being unwanted, then well, let's be honest, don't do the deed that may result in a child. Or have surgery to make it impossible, if it is economically burdensome. The big one that is a problem, is the one where the child is being aborted by another child. We live in a world where children are having sexual relations way too much and way too early. I know all of what I just said sounds prudish and old-fashioned like I don't understand the times. No. I understand it all too well. Just because our ideas (values) about sex have changed, does not mean those new ideas are correct and moral. And there is the problem with abortion. It is not that we have them, but we feel we *need* them for some immoral reasons based on man's values and not the foundation of God.

If we think there is too much racism out there (which there is) we feel like laws will stop it. Now, how can a law stop hatred? In mid-2020 I heard Congress had to pass a law making lynching a federal crime (H.R. 35). Seriously? Why was it not a federal crime before this? Yes, it's a hate crime. It's murder. This is a no-brainer of a law. It's a common- sense law for which I am all for. Believe it or not, it was not unanimous. The vote was 410-4. But will the law stop the hatred? No. Will any law stop anyone from hating someone else? No. The problem is not with not having enough laws making racism illegal but it's our culture, the village, that is still filled with hate. We have to change the hearts of people, not create thousands of laws. If we had less hate, we would have less need for any law dealing with hate. And why do we have this hate in our world? We have it because God is no longer the foundation.

In all of these cases that have been discussed, the issue is not the *topic* for which we created laws. The issue is the *reasoning* we have used in creating the laws. The issue is our culture. Our culture now has the wrong foundation. This will be discussed later on in the book. If your foundation is wrong, then no matter what you do, there will always be issues. My point through all of this, is that the culture should not define who we are; we should define the culture. The culture should not limit families. Families should limit the culture. Cultures need to be based on the family. The family should not be based on the culture. The culture needs the family to be a structured base. The family needs God as its foundation. It doesn't take a Proverbial village to raise a child. It takes a Proverbial good foundation with the right structure!

Proverbs 22:6, (ESV)

*"Train up a child in the way he **should** go; even when he is old he will not depart from it."*

The key word is "should." If you teach a child the way God wants you to, then he or she will not suffer the derangement from the culture. We no longer teach children the way they *should* go. We are not acting like parents. We let the streets teach them. We allow the culture to raise our children. We let the village and the village idiot help raise our child. The village thinks they know better than the parents. The village thinks they know more than God. The only way they can do that is if they take the children and put them into groups. *Groups.* And then we wonder why the world is the way it is.

5
Solidarity but Separate

When I was younger getting a box of crayons was the greatest thing ever. Seeing all the bright colors, and knowing my world of imagination was about to take off, was the greatest feeling. Those eight colors allowed me to create a world that would believe in me and that I could control. But when I got a 16-count box or the ultimate prize, the 64-count box, I was in heaven. I didn't know what to do with so many colors. But I knew I could do more than color with them, and I did. I used to separate them into "like" colors. Reds and light reds on one side. Blues of all types on the other. And still greens and yellows and browns all around in their own little piles. What did I do with them besides color? I made them have war with each other. I divided them based on their color and pretended they had war. The only way to get rid of the war was when I was done and put them all together again in the same box (still separated though in the box). I did the same with my Star Wars action figures. The only way they all stood a chance to have peace, was to be united back together. The same with the real world, or at least it's how the world thinks. Now that we have seen the breakdown of the culture, in this chapter let's see how the culture has tried to fix the problems it created.

The world's goal from a humanistic standpoint is to become one. Globalization seems to be the new standard we are trying to achieve. Its actual meaning started out as how the world started to depend upon each other for trade. But in the last few decades, it has taken on a broader meaning. It now has incorporated social systems and humanitarian activity, as well as economic activity to bring the world together. Globalization and humanism are very much intertwined. We have made the world smaller with all of the technology. We can travel faster. We can communicate faster. We can build faster, trade faster, and anything else you can think of; we can do it faster. But it is odd. Even though the world, and even the universe, is smaller we have never had so many barriers that separate us farther apart than ever before.

It seems like the more people that we have in this world and the closer that we have to live together, due to overpopulation, the more groups we have been separated into and the farther apart we actually have become. Another major aspect of our culture is the need to feel we should be divided into groups for some reason, like I did with crayons. Everywhere we look we have groups, sects, or some kind of division. Our culture is filled with groups, and these groups are perhaps a negative aspect of our existence.

Groups, in and of themselves, are not bad. Groups can allow us to feel like we are part of something. There are great groups like Boy Scouts and Girl Scouts, support groups, sports teams, workforces, intellectual groups, and the military. Groups can give us things to discuss that we all may believe in or enjoy like book clubs, television show parties, and fan clubs. They give us support when we need it like AA, eating disorders groups, abuse networks, and the like. Some groups are natural, such as your racial makeup. Some groups have become natural over time, like ethnicity. Some groups have become natural over time, and through choice, like your nationality. The culture may need some of these groups. And as I said, the group itself may not be a bad idea. But not all groups are positive.

In the past, there have been groups that were created that have given us positive progress in society. They have started movements that have gotten things changed. New innovations and inventions have been created by some groups. Groups have given us a sense of solidarity. When we stick together, we have strength in numbers, and we can get things accomplished. Even a famous motto from Alexandre Dumas' *The Three Musketeers* is something most of us believe in, "All for one and one for all." But there is also another saying that has been attributed to Aesop in one of his fables, which is just as true as the *The Three Musketeers* quote; "United we stand, divided we fall." Both ring true that we are always better when we are together. Division never helps. Groups divide us.

Groups may bring us some positive progression, but they tend to divide us too much. An example is that our sports teams give us the feeling that we are being a part of something. It could also cause such a severe rivalry that things can get out of control. Honduras and El Salvador went to war over a soccer game in July 1969. Granted it was only for 100 hours, but still. Groups can unfortunately give us certain identities that way too many people take to heart. Many times, the groups that we belong to end up becoming our only identity. I know a few people who, all they talk about are the group that they identify with. A person who was and in most ways is still very dear to me always makes sure that he tells people what sports team he likes. His friends are all about this team. His conversations usually ended up talking about this team. After a while, it becomes a little irritating. I even started to hate this team, just based on the number of conversations I would hear about them. Another certain person in my life is all about being homosexual. That is what the whole universe boils down to with her. She feels people "don't like her," because of her homosexuality. Over the years her hair changed. Her clothes changed. Her attitude towards her family changed. She became isolated in life, all because of her homosexuality. It's all she became. It was her only identity. And for the life of me, I can't remember any of us ever talking out loud about that aspect of her life, when we were all together unless she brought it up. I am sure there were private conversations, and from what I understand those were about others trying to understand her feelings and why she became this way, (isolated that is), not why she became homosexual. But we never separated this person from us. She did it on her own.

Groups give us a feeling of belonging and identity when we feel alone. Such as, gangs are groups. People in gangs use this connection as their main identity. When I first started teaching, gangs had entered the local city that I lived in. Students wouldn't talk to each other if they were in opposing gangs. Group work was out of the question. Students told me I had to watch what I said because words now meant something different. I told them no one was going to change my vocabulary and that I was only teaching lessons, not getting involved or taking sides. They became very defensive while they were in school. The papers I would try and grade were full of nonsense. For those who were in the "crips", they would spell things incorrectly on purpose because it might be against their gang. Such as if they were writing the word "click" they would write it "clicc" because when you had a C and K together it represented "crip killer," and crips would not put those together. I even had a young lady who was brilliant, but was lost to a gang and changed the spelling of her own name to fit in with the crips. It got ridiculous. But gangs separated these young people into a hatred for each other that absolutely had no real meaning in life. Colors and clothes were representing them as if they actually mattered as life or death. Shoe brands and sporting teams also became a matter of life and death. Unfortunately, it did become a matter of life and death. Gangs kill over colors and shoes.

There are all kinds of groups we could use as examples. I think having some groups is a good thing. But when groups start to divide us and not give us something to believe in together, then they are in opposition to what they are supposed to be doing. They tear us apart and do not bring us together. I will show you this in a little while. By far the three largest types of groups that separate us the most are race, religion, and politics.

RACE, ETHNICITY, AND NATIONALITY DIVISION

I don't like it but I can understand why religion does it to us. Religious beliefs are our deepest thoughts and beliefs, and if someone disagrees with those it is very personal. That is not to say that I agree with the division, nor do I like the division. I can just understand it. But religion has divided us so much in this world, that there have been many wars where religion was a factor. As a Christian, I am ashamed of the fact that we had the Crusades (a common atheist argument about how unloving Christians are, and a reason they use to "prove" there is no God). Those who went to war and killed people in the Crusades were wrong. The Spanish Inquisition was wrong. However, on the other side, the Moors, Seljuks, and Ottoman Empire were also wrong in what they did during these times as well. But keep in mind, that wars are also fought by atheists over religion. Atheists are not any more innocent in this type of mess than believers are. Leaders who were atheists such as Joseph Stalin and Mao Zedong, caused mass murders of their own people and even genocide. Stalin practiced killing based on people being anti-religious. He killed the Christians in Ukraine who stood up to him during what is now called the Holodomor. In the United States, we have freedom of religion, but that freedom has caused more issues than some of the wars. Atheists have used this freedom to also include freedom *from* religion; which in reality the First Amendment would support that idea. But the idea of what religious freedom is has caused so much turmoil in the United States. Does freedom mean religion can be taught in school? Does freedom mean any belief can be practiced, even if human sacrifice is involved? Then again, does it mean atheists can remove all religious items from public places? Does it mean that Christians can pray in school? I know what to do about it. Let's create laws to make that decision!

In the last 30 years or so the proverbial pendulum has swung way to the atheist side of the argument. In a democracy, they may have a point, but the people in that democracy could still have God as a foundation somehow and still be a democracy. Democracy is part of a culture, but let's remind ourselves of something here from earlier chapters. The culture should be driven by families, and families should be grounded in God, whether atheists want it to or not. But unfortunately, religion is not the only major thing that divides us. Some are natural differences but still shouldn't divide us. The natural groups that we have are those that divide us by our race, ethnicity, or nationality. These three are not the same thing. I guess to understand this part we need to define what these are.

Your race is your genetic background. These are your facial features, your body structure, and your DNA. This is what separates us due to our skin color. It's a completely stupid reason to be separated but we are. If you are a Christian then having any kind of hatred in this area is very unChrist-like. Adam and Eve were one. All races came from them. Over time adaptation to the climate and resources and evolution (but NOT in the Darwinian classical sense) have made us look different. Noah had three sons. They married three women. The genetic makeup of all the races was found in them too somehow, some way as well, either through Noah's sons and/or their wives. We are all one people. But for some reason, we choose to separate ourselves because of what we see or don't see in the mirror. And if you are not Christian and still feel some racist idea then you're lost in more ways than one. Your race does not or at least should not define who you are. It does not or at least should never mean you are a certain way or should be treated differently. Your race just means what you look like. But in the world today, race has become a major factor in deciding customs, traditions, and laws; a far fetch from what race means. I can't dress a certain way, because it would be cultural misappropriation. Even though it may be the color that enhances my eyes, I would not be allowed, due to groups not liking it. Now it would be different if I did it to make fun of a culture or race, but why would I not be allowed to look the way I want?

Your ethnicity is not your color. It has nothing to do with your color. Your ethnicity has nothing to do with the borders you live between, although many borders have been drawn for those reasons. Your ethnicity is the distinction of your ancestral traditions. It's the food you are accustomed to. It's the music you traditionally listen to. It's the clothing. It's many times your language. Your ethnicity is a learned behavior over time. Hispanics are not just Mexican. They are not just Colombian. They are not just Cuban. Hispanics share common foods, language, and dance but Hispanics make up at least three different races. There are black Hispanics. There are white Hispanics. There are mixed Hispanics. The majority are probably Native American Hispanics. If Spain had controlled the Philippines longer, we might be calling some Asians even Hispanic. The Spanish Empire set up colonies south of Texas and forced the people into the Spanish culture such as what England did to North American indigenous people. In Africa, there are many different ethnicities with at least three races. In northern Africa, you have Arabic and some Caucasian. In central Africa, you have rainforest peoples and savannah peoples such as the Bantu speakers. In southern Africa due to imperialism, you have a mixture. In Europe, there are many ethnicities with at least two races, mostly although only one in the main part of Europe; the Caucasian. In the United States, we have the most ethnicities. This is where we get the great melting pot theory. However, many would say we are more of a salad bowl. We haven't mixed as much as the melting pot would imply. We are still very much divided by our ethnicities. Ethnicity is where most of your country's customs and traditions come from. It is also where we get some of the traditions that divide us too much. We have ethnic holidays that are respected and some only celebrate either due to being invited or some ulterior motive. Here is what I mean. Those of mostly European backgrounds would probably not celebrate their daughter's 15th birthday. However, if you were Hispanic, you would more than likely have a *quinceañera*. If you were of African descent, somehow you would more than likely not celebrate *Oktoberfest* unless you really liked beer. Most ethnic groups don't worry about other ethnic group celebrations because they are localized. But notice when there are groups that separate themselves to celebrate in front of the world, that is when we have issues. There is nothing wrong with Black History Month, but it automatically divides us. There is Hispanic Heritage Month. There is Irish Heritage Month. These groups have parades. They have festivals. They celebrate publicly and in front of the world. Some of these actually interfere with the rest of the community. They will shut down downtown areas to celebrate a certain group. They will close off local parks. They will rent out amusement parks and the rest of us have to let it go. Groups start to splinter off from the main culture and we start to have problems within the country. Sometimes these groups try to form their own nationality.

Your nationality is simply the nation you feel you belong to. Nationality is where your government and laws come from. Your borders are not always the same as your nation of allegiance. Native Americans are citizens of the United States, yet they are also their own nation. Sometimes people within a country do not feel like they belong. Some regions such as Quebec in Canada, Catalonia in Spain, and Tibet in China, are actually nations, but they are controlled by another country and its laws. If given the right chance and circumstances these nations may try and secede from the country that controls them. Quebec in 1995 had a referendum on whether to stay with Canada or secede. Scotland did the same thing with the United Kingdom in 2014. Neither left. This is what I was referring to earlier in Chapter 4, and nationalism. The feeling of nationalism can unite a country if the people in that nation can focus on what they have in common. If the people are divided, then they may choose to break away and form a new nation. Americans in the 1700s were British in their ethnicity. We had a few races here. We even had a few different origins of nationalities, but they became one. We became British. We spoke English. We drank tea. We had a king. Even if you were a slave and forced to do it, English became your culture. Some from other ethnicities Anglicized their names, such as the Martinez family may have become the Martins. Even my family name was Hertzog but that would be weird in English so the "T" was dropped, making it less weird. Americans fought for the British up until the day we said no more. We became our own nation and we started to develop our own culture. Although, we are still divided in many ways.

Wars have been started over nationalities (over land). Wars have been started over ethnicities (over desires, religions, and traditions). There have not been that many wars started over race. Yes, there have been wars where two sides may be racially different but compared to all the other wars not many are over just a racial issue. Racial fighting is internal to a country and is a sign of a cultural breakdown. Unfortunately, internal racial fighting has turned into genocide. Racial differences tear into the heart of a country. Politicians use this all the time to gain an advantage for their personal agendas.

POLITICAL DIVISIONS

Many groups divide us. We could create pages of groups that do. But by far the one type of group that probably escalates all of our division the most, would be politics. Politics has always been a nasty and dirty thing. I was having a conversation with a teacher colleague during a "professional development" day, and we got onto the topic of politics. He mentioned the word liar and I stopped him and said that liar and politician were the same words. I was joking when I said this (for the most) but a local union leader of my school district overheard and stepped in and tried to say how wrong I was. So, I asked her then which politician is not a liar. She responded by naming six different people, all from the same political party. I guess only one party was truthful and the others, especially one other, were the liars. Unions are very political and are groups that have divided us; again, that's another book.

George Washington may not have been the perfect person. You can research on your own about him and his life. As president, he was the best one we have ever had and none can be rightfully compared. He brought up out of the dust a country that went through war and was ready to waste away after that war, only to become the first leader of eventually the strongest country in history. He set precedents and was respected in his stature, military, and leadership. He warned us not to get involved with worldly issues and their troubles. The most important thing he said was, "However [political parties] may now and then answer popular ends, they are likely in the course of time and things, to become potent engines, by which cunning, ambitious, and unprincipled men will be enabled to subvert the power of the people and to usurp for themselves the reins of government, destroying afterward the very engines which have lifted them to unjust dominion." (George Washington, 1796) He warned us not to have political parties. These groups may offer short-term answers but over time they will manipulate and control those who allowed them to become the leaders. Politics control all the other groups. The Democrats and Republicans and those who adhere religiously to their party lines are the biggest dividers there are, especially the last five presidents. President Clinton who did not give respect to President Bush (41) during the debates is an example. He called him "Mr. Bush" instead of "Mr. President". Later on, his pompousness and arrogance took away the integrity of the office. He was impeached. And if you know why he was impeached, you see where it got him. When President Bush (43) took over after President Clinton and the whole Iraq/WMD ordeal went down, it got worse. People felt like they couldn't trust the office of the president. Then when President Obama took over, he used racial issues as a new way of division and allowed his narcissism to shine through. Being biracial and having a few racial matters rise up during his presidency, he had the perfect opportunity to do something about it and heal the nation. He did not. He further divided the people with his speeches, although he would never admit to that due to his narcissism. President Trump intimidated anyone opposing him with all the Twitter nonsense, name-calling, threats of lawsuits, and accusations. He is another president who had the opportunity to heal the nation but his rhetoric Twitter wars and his promises to stop groups with force have now pretty much broken our culture almost to the end. People turned to President Biden for a change. Impotence. We may be one but we are still divided. Maybe there is hope in each person, the individual.

6

Don't Tread on Me

FREEDOM OF THE INDIVIDUAL

I have had over 5000 students in my teaching career. Sometimes there are students who look like former students, and the similarities are amazing. They say everyone has a twin, and science may have proven that. In 2003 the famous human genome project was finished. It was a study to find out how to map and put into sequence all of our DNA. One of the lead investors and biotechnologists of the project was Craig Venter. When much of the research was finished, he was known to have said, "We are all essentially identical twins." Backing his view is another scientist, Kenneth Kidd. He said, "Race is not biologically definable, we are far too similar." In other words, the human race is definitely one large group. We all come from the same beginning. We are so similar we are 99.9% identical. (James F. Crow, 2002) Yet, we can still see all kinds of hair color, eye color, height, shape, noses, and metabolism. Even more so, we can witness differences in our attitudes and personalities that make us totally unique. So, if 0.1% can create all these differences physically, then imagine how many different outcomes of situations there can be when we add our personalities. Humanism stresses human individuality and the right to live how you want, because "what is right for you may not be right for some." Everyone is right in their own way. How can every individual be right?

The top tier of our structure is the individual. The individual is what it all comes down to. Does the individual do what they are supposed to do, or do they do the wrong thing? Do they allow the culture to drive them? Do they have the right beliefs? Do they have the right foundation? Do they start their existence with themselves or do they start it with a strong foundation? We will see in this chapter how the individual has been affected by the breakdown of our culture.

The biggest issue for any individual is how much freedom they have. Individuals make decisions. These decisions direct our course of action. Our actions are what make us or break us. The one thing we have to stress here is that the individual is responsible for all his or her actions. No one in normal circumstances can force you to do anything. Normal means making decisions in everyday situations. Someone holding a gun to your head telling you to do something is not a normal situation. Living with mental disabilities is not a normal situation. Being a child who does not understand certain things in life is a normal situation, but they should not be held accountable for certain actions due to their age. Your race, nationality, creed, religion, ethnicity, or adult age should not be an excuse for *any* action. I would even venture to say that even the fears, abuses, or neglect of your childhood are still no excuse for your actions unless they seriously caused some mental instability. But all of that aside, you alone are responsible for your actions.

The Bible clearly talks about how at the end of our lives we will be judged according to our deeds.

Matthew 12:36, (NIV)

"But I tell you that everyone will have to give account on the day of judgment for every empty word they have spoken."

Other verses you can look up are 1 Corinthians 4:5, Hebrews 9:27, and Revelation 20:11-5 to name a few. However, if you are Christian, your price was paid for by Jesus. Since He died for you, then you will be judged according to Him and His actions, not yours. He was perfect. You are forgiven and saved by Grace. Anyway, this book is about humanity not about our eternity, so I will move on.

An individual is free but is bound by the other parts of our structure. For example, you make your own decisions but your decisions cannot be against the law. You still have to follow society's rules. We still live in communities, and you just can't do anything you want. You make your own decisions but have a responsibility to the community and your family. You need to take responsibility for your children. You just can't let them run all over the place unruly and hurt other people. It will in the end hurt them as well. You need to teach them how to live in society. You should not dishonor your family. And you most certainly should not go against the moral standards that God laid down. You need to live a life that will bear good fruit. God wanted you to be free but not antisocial or psychotic, like Cain. He wanted you to make your own decisions but He wanted you to make decisions that will be for the good of the order and not be selfish.

HUMAN ESSENCE AND THE INDIVIDUAL

As stated in Chapter 1, the individual is in charge of his or her beliefs and actions. You have a choice in how you make your decisions. You can be driven by your senses. You can be driven by your intellect. Or you could be driven by your spirit. Whichever way you decide to be driven will change your outcome. Each part of your essence can drive you into different pathways. And we need to choose the right way to think and respond. This is not to say that all your senses or intellect are wrong to have or to indulge in, but it has to be in the right situation. Below shows the differences between our essences and what they are used for in our lives.

Figure 9
The Essence of the Human Existence

Body	Soul	Spirit
❑Reason: to interact with the physical world	❑Reason: to interact with the other souls	❑Reason: to interact with the God
❑Relationship: Sensual (Eros)	❑Relationship: Emotional (Phileo)	❑Relationship: Worship (Agape)
❑Reaction: fight or flight	❑Reaction: reason or imagine	❑Reaction: faith or conviction
❑Refinement: touch, smell, feel, hear, and sight, physical health	❑Refinement: ideas, beliefs, feelings, attitudes, demeanors, mental health, personality	❑Refinement: dreams, hopes, discernment, purpose, born again (spiritual health)
❑Result: wants to fulfill the desire of the senses	❑Result: wants to connect to others and feel a belonging	❑Result: wants to do the right things

Source: My old blog website, www.ideasoftimbible.blogspot.com

Sometimes we make our decisions based on what we see, feel, hear, and even taste or smell. When we make these decisions based on these things, it is what the Bible in Romans calls living by the flesh. This is not the way we were meant to live. If we live by the flesh, we will almost always make the wrong decision.

Romans 8:13, (Berean Study Bible)

"For if you live according to the flesh, you will die;
but if by the Spirit you put to death the deeds of the
body, you will live."

Our eyes can deceive us. Our ears can cause fear by what we hear. The touch of flesh can give us inappropriate feelings. When we live by the flesh, we tend to make decisions on the spur of the moment. We live in the moment, and we usually pay for it later. This is when we hurt others. Living by the flesh means we become very selfish. We live for our own wants and desires. We become a little hedonistic, in a way. We become worldly and throw away the moral standard of God. We become secular and start to rely upon the flesh. We then get into the wrong kind of relationship. The relationships that we end up being in are superficial. They are based on what the Greeks would call *eros*. *Eros* is based on appearance and stimulation. Beauty only goes so far. Those relationships are built on vanity. They are short-term relationships because once we look deeper, we realize there is nothing there and we remain empty. Those who go from this type of relationship to the next will never feel fulfilled in life. We make sure we only fight for ourselves. We become impulsive and speak before we think. Now I don't know how smell and taste can mess with us but I am sure there has to be something out there. Esau after all gave up his birthright just for the taste of stew. The point is that all created flesh has weak points, and if we live by the flesh, then we will always come up short. Why do humanists think we can be saved by human actions and intellect?

Sometimes, and probably most of the time, we make decisions based on our intellect. The issue that lies with that, is the level of our intellect! Some will never make it if that is all they rely upon. Let's face it. Turn on the news and you see the stupidity of the locals. Turn on TV shows like ABC's "America's Funniest Home Video" or MTV's "Ridiculousness," and you wonder how the human race has made it this far. And I do admit I indulge myself in these shows every once in a while. On the other hand, some people who rely upon their intellect are just too smart for their own britches. Many of my arguments on those internet forums mentioned earlier include the phrase "Prove your God exists" way too many times. In all reality, we can never prove, using science and human standards, that God exists to the point that atheists will believe. Even if you had actual physical evidence of God, the atheist would find some excuse not to believe. One time (more than once even on the same internet thread) I was having a conversation about miracles and how I prayed for my father to be healed of cancer. My father had what they had diagnosed as a very progressive form of cancer, anaplastic thyroid cancer, stage 4. They gave him only 6 months to live. We had him anointed with oil and prayed over him. When they got him to the operating table, they quickly changed their diagnosis and said it was an early stage of a different kind of cancer, non-Hodgkin's large-cell lymphoma. As of today, he has lived 15 years longer than what was expected. When I told an atheist this story, he called me a liar. Another one on the same thread of the forum said there had to be a scientific reason why that happened, such as doctor error, and that prayer did nothing for the situation. Another one just complained that since God didn't heal everyone with cancer it wasn't that big of a deal. They want evidence in their own way, but if that happens and they get their evidence, they would change the perimeter of the evidence needed. As you can see from Figure 9, the intellect can be driven by reasoning. They want God right in front of them, right now. The problem with that is God was here once before when He came as Jesus and stood in front of many people and a lot of them didn't believe Him then either, even with all of the miracles He did. The Atheist doesn't need evidence. They need help.

THE ATHEIST/HUMANIST INTELLECT

Atheists and Humanists only want scientific reasoning; human reasoning that stems from human experience. Everything has to be proven to them. They get very angry when you point out that they cannot disprove God either. They will always spout out with something like, "You can't prove a negative." So, I then say God is not a negative but you also can't prove all "positive" things anyway. Such as love. What is love? Can you prove it? You can prove what it does. You can talk about how it causes chemical reactions and causes us to do things. But you cannot say what it actually is. Yet, it is real. I searched online for science and love. I found this interesting article from www.atheist- faq.com. The same question about proving love was posed to them. Listen to the response. "First, we need to clarify what it means to "prove" something. Science doesn't prove anything to an absolute degree - that's not possible outside of mathematics. Instead, "proving" something translates into "demonstration beyond a reasonable doubt," as long as we're open to revision down the road…Science also doesn't require direct observation…It's faster, but not required. The Rutherford Gold Foil Experiment, for example, was an experiment that simply was trying to determine whether atoms had distinct nuclei or not. We couldn't "see" the atomic nucleus, but we could still indirectly test for it. Much of science operates in this way. "Unseen" phenomena are not insurmountable problems for science."

Let's stop there and see what has been said so far. If someone tells you to prove God scientifically, tell them science, according to this atheist, doesn't prove things-- only math does. So, let's see if it adds up. Give them all that is in Chapter 2 to start with. The writer said we need to be open to revision down the road. The atheists I speak to are never open to God being "down the road." The last part is great. Unseen phenomena are not a problem for science because they don't have to see things to test for it, yet God has to be seen or He isn't real. Stop me if I am wrong, but isn't one of the major steps to the scientific method, observation? Why does God have to be seen for proof but unseen phenomena don't?

Back to the article. "If you go to a park, during a nice summer's day with people around, are you able to determine who's in love, or who is angry or sad? Most people can, and it's because the phenomenon of love is giving off evidence. A consistent set of patterns surrounds each emotion…Love isn't in the same category as physical objects…Few people dispute that Microsoft Windows exists… but you can't see it, or touch it. All you can do is interact with it through an interface - the monitor, keyboard, mouse, etc. What's displayed on the monitor could be just an illusion by another program…Yet, we consider interacting through this interface to be sufficient to demonstrate its existence."

They can't see love but they can see it giving off the evidence. You can't see Microsoft Windows but you can interact with it.

Love isn't in the same category as physical objects. Now that is the one thing they really got right. God is love. This love is not in the same category. We may not see Him but we can interact with Him. And we most certainly can see Him giving off evidence. But their intellect gets in the way.

Back to the article. "The same applies to emotions. The person's actions, body language, speech, facial expressions, etc. are all "the interface," and most people are fairly good at accurately detecting another person's mood on a basic level... Science "proves" through hypothesis-testing, and the scientific field of Psychology has countless studies on love alone, controlling for different variables, setting up blinded trials, etc. Further, when we examine the brain from a biological perspective, we find empirical evidence of altered brain chemistry from love. We've found increased production of the Nerve Growth Factor in people who are first in love. Specific regions of the brain have increased activity when people experience love, as CAT/MRI scans demonstrate, to the point that we're learning the specific nuances of the phenomenon, from a biological stance...Science has long since moved on from trying to demonstrate that love exists, and is busy figuring out precisely how it works. If the existence of a god were as easy to demonstrate as love, this website wouldn't exist. *(See resource page.)*

To be honest, they should have gotten someone else to answer the question if they wanted to prove, I mean, demonstrate beyond a reasonable doubt that this is accurate. Not once did they answer the question. Can love be proven? This article tried to deflect the real question. They talked about why they couldn't do it. They talked about what love does. They talked about how they aren't trying to prove it anyway because they know they can't do it. Yet, they will fight to the end that God can never be proven and that apparently His effects on us are not the same "empirical evidence" that love has. Do you see what I mean now about how some are too smart for their britches? This is why we cannot rely upon human reasoning, the same reasoning the individual has without a foundation in God.

Living by the mind and intellect will always leave you short. The relationships that we see come out of those who rely upon their intellect are emotional and very competitive. They are more worried about who is right and who is wrong on a subject, not morally, just factually. This is not to say that the relationship won't last. They actually can be very fulfilling. But I personally would question if the love between them is true. This type of love I would consider as the *phileo* kind. *Phileo* is a conditional type of love. There is some kind of condition placed upon the relationship. People will have a certain connection. The love between them is mutual but not complete. They connect with the mind but their dreams may not be connected. Some will tend to focus more on their own career than the relationship. What happens when their dreams and foundations are based on different things? Will they stay on the same path or will the competition cause them to drift apart? Love only works when two people can share more than just looks, ideas, and dreams. There has to be a stronger force connecting them. Paul told us in Corinthians what that means.

2 Corinthians 6:14, (Amp)

> *"Do not be unequally bound together with unbelievers [do not make mismatched alliances with them, inconsistent with your faith]. For what partnership can righteousness have with lawlessness? Or what fellowship can light have with darkness?"*

This piece of scripture is a warning to make sure your foundations are the same. Now if two intellectuals have the same foundation then their marriage will work, but they would still be lost when it comes to *complete* love; there will always be a hole in their life. And if they rely upon their intellect, they will never fill that void because they won't know the void is God. Having the *same* foundation does not mean having the *right* foundation. You need the right foundation.

So, if all you do is try to live life with just your intellect you will always come up short. Human intellect is not perfect.

1 Corinthians 1:27, (Christian Standard Bible)

"Instead, God has chosen what is foolish in the world to shame the wise, and God has chosen what is weak in the world to shame the strong."

Remember the intellect of mankind; the ones who have thousands of wars, cause millions to be infected with incurable contagious diseases, abuse children, have racism, cheat, lie, steal, allow hunger, and so forth. You know, *that* intellect. Yes, there are many things we discovered, but we had to *discover* them with our intellect. God had already *created* them without our help. There is nothing wrong with being smart. As a teacher I highly recommend it, but we have to understand that our intellect is not perfect and it is limited. When we live by our intellect, we become blind to things that do not make sense to us. We become arrogant and think we know it all.

THE SPIRITUAL INTELLECT

But when we live by the spirit, we stop to think. We stop life to weigh our decisions to see if they are morally upright. We think of others to make sure that our actions will be good for the whole situation and not just for a moment. We think of others to make sure their lives are not hurt. And we think of ourselves to make sure our relationship with God is correct.

I used to work at a rehabilitation center for teens. We had times each day when each resident had to explain why they were there, called their "cycle" if I remember correctly. They would go through the day that they were arrested and explain to the group what they were thinking as they committed the crime and then state why what they did was wrong. When I sat in on the discussions some things kept coming up in each one of their cycles. They saw an opportunity to do something and they just did it without thinking about their actions. They didn't care about the consequences, because they didn't think about any consequences. They only cared about what they would get out of it. When we live by the flesh we don't think of the future. When we live by the intellect, we think of the future but only subjectively. When we live by the spirit, we think of the future because we can make a true discernment of right and wrong, subjectively and morally speaking. Those will be statements that the atheist, the humanist, and the liberal will detest.

The relationships will not just be built upon attraction. They will be more than intellectual stimulation. There will be a deeper connection between the people. This is not to say that Christians will always have a better relationship because not all Christians live by the spirit. They get caught up in the flesh and intellect just as much as anyone else. But when I was dating my wife, we were first attracted to each other physically. Her beauty inside and out made me so anxious I couldn't get the nerve to ask her out for a year. But after the first few dates, I got beyond the physical attraction as a reason to like her. I started to learn who she was and how her mind worked. But we did have one more thing in common that solidified our relationship. We met at church. We both had a foundation within us, due to our parents. It just wasn't a common foundation; it was the right one. If by chance she only built the relationship on my pure masculinity (hear the sarcasm please), then what happened when I lost my hair? If we only based our relationship on our intellect, then what happened if she disagreed with me? Long story short, we have been together 30 years now because the foundation allowed us to build our relationship on something more beyond my handsome ruggedness and intelligence quotient, not to mention my extravagant humbleness.

What I am trying to say in all of this is that the individual's beliefs and actions are the result of our structure. The culture may tell us what is right and wrong in the eyes of that culture, and we are responsible for listening. The individual learns from the family and is taught the values that drive our beliefs. Individuals need to have the strongest foundation and the right foundation. And from the beginning, it has never changed, that foundation is God. Any other foundation will crumble on its own.

7

The Breakdown

THE FOUNDATION HAS CRUMBLED

When things used to break at my parent's home, the first thing my dad tried to use to repair it was duct tape. Anything that broke automatically got the duct tape treatment. Table broke? Duct tape. Washer and dryer broken? Duct tape. Window pane broke? Duct tape. Car seat torn? Duct tape. We became accustomed to it so much that when the VCR broke, my three-year-old nephew ran and got the duct tape for him to use. He didn't want to buy new stuff to replace the broken parts, he just tried to use a substitute. Eventually, those items would just get other things wrong to them because it wasn't fixed right. The rest of the machine couldn't handle the stress that was put on it due to the broken part. And of course, the inevitable fate of that item happened over time; it became useless. Now, later on in life he rigged things up and invented some of the strangest things that actually worked, up to the point that my uncle thought he was a genius. But that is a different story. Of course, it goes without saying the "fixed" items never worked as well as the original item. Duct tape or any kind of substitution will never replace the original item or foundation. The original foundation is the best.

Now that we have seen the structure (Figure 2) and why we should have a foundation that is built upon God, let's see what has happened because we no longer, as a people, live by this moral structure. Humanism has taken over and has destroyed the true foundation. Our foundation in the United States has now changed. It used to be based on Christian values. Yes, it was. Humanism has created a new foundation, but one that has caused the culture to be so divided it cannot and will not stand.

Our foundation has crumbled. Over the years God has become less and less important in our society. God is no longer found in our mainstream society. When your foundation loses its importance, the rest of the structure is weakened. That is true in all things, even literal buildings. When searching for a home, check the foundation before anything else. If the foundation is good then the rest of the house has a chance. If the foundation is shot, then do not even think about buying that house. God even prophesied this foundation for us in a few places.

Isaiah 28:16, (NIV)

"So this is what the Sovereign LORD says: 'See, I lay a stone in Zion, a tested stone, a precious cornerstone for a sure foundation; the one who relies on it will never be stricken with panic.'"

God laid the foundation. God sent Jesus to remind us and to be that foundation for us. But look what He said would happen.

Psalms 118:22, (multiple versions)

"The stone that the builders rejected has become the cornerstone."

Jesus will be rejected. He is the foundation but He will be rejected. Jesus then reminded the people of His time and warned them about what would happen because of the rejection.

Luke 20:17-18, (ESV)

But he looked directly at them and said, "What then is this that is written: The stone that the builders rejected has become the cornerstone'? Everyone who falls on that stone will be broken to pieces, and when it falls on anyone, it will crush him."

If we fall on the stone, which means we are pretending to be on the foundation, then we will not stay together. The religious leaders pretended to be righteous. Rome crushed Jerusalem 40 years later. If we reject the foundation (it falls on us) then we will be crushed and fall apart. We need to *build* on that foundation. We need to stick to the morals of God. But we have now rejected Him and look at what has happened to this country; extremism and division. The right and original foundation is broken. And just like a building that has its foundation broken, the rest of the structure has cracks in it and can no longer be supported correctly. The family has broken apart. As seen in Figure 5 back in Chapter 3, there are less than 30% of families that are strong and filled with love. If the family lost its foundation and has cracks in it then that crack expands into the culture. Our culture has become immoral and divided and is now starting to break apart. And because of all of that, the individual is hurting now more than at any other time in history. Another question I ask the students in the end-of-the-year survey is "Are you happy in life." Anywhere between 5-10% always say no. Only about 15% say yes. That means basically 70%

of the world just lives to survive day to day, like an animal. The individual is hurting because they are not living the full life they were meant to be living.

WHAT WAS DESTROYED?

There is a huge argument if the United States was built upon religious freedom and the Judeo-Christian value system or not. The argument is over. We were. Case closed. The first ones who came to this part of the world, which would eventually create a new nation, came here during the English Civil War; the same civil war that brought Cromwell to power. This civil war was between a Catholic King James and a Protestant law-making body called Parliament, the Roundheads. Yes, it was a stupid war based on a ridiculous separation since both Catholics and Protestants are Christ- based. But those who fled the situation, left because they did not want to be controlled religiously. The Puritans came over on the *Mayflower* in 1620 to escape the situation. The Mayflower Compact is known as the first American governing document. Here is the document in its entirety:

> *"IN THE NAME OF GOD, AMEN. We, whose names are underwritten, the Loyal Subjects of our dread Sovereign Lord King James, by the Grace of God, of Great Britain, France, and Ireland, King, Defender of the Faith, and having undertaken for the Glory of God, and Advancement of the Christian Faith, and the Honour of our King and Country, a Voyage to plant the first Colony in the northern Parts of Virginia; Do by these Presents, solemnly and mutually, in the Presence of God and one another, covenant and*

combine ourselves together into a civil Body Politick, for our better Ordering and Preservation, and Furtherance of the Ends aforesaid: And by Virtue hereof do enact, constitute, and frame, such just and equal Laws, Ordinances, Acts, Constitutions, and Officers, from time to time, as shall be thought most meet and convenient for the general Good of the Colony; unto which we promise all due Submission and Obedience.

IN WITNESS whereof we have hereunto subscribed our names at Cape-Cod the eleventh of November, in the Reign of our Sovereign Lord King James, of England, France, and Ireland, the eighteenth, and of Scotland the fifty-fourth, Anno Domini; 1620."

This group combined the freedom of people with the foundation of God. This country was built on that foundation. Now it is true that later on, we add secularism and even things like Masonic and Deistic ideas into it all, a major mistake if you ask me. But the argument is over. The problem is now we have rejected that cornerstone. One hundred fifty years later after this agreement, the United States was created. And even though the laws never mention God, the laws that we had were made by people who had a Christian background for the most or at least had an idea of God. The main document that showed the world what we wanted *does* mention God and that further settles the whole argument.

The Declaration of Independence, 1776, states:

"We hold these truths to be self-evident, that all men are created equal, that they are endowed by their Creator with certain unalienable Rights, that among these are Life, Liberty and the pursuit of Happiness."

What do the naysayers think the "Creator" is? So, now that we understand the country did have a foundation in the Christian God (although again many were Deists only) we can now discuss what has happened since. Deism means they believe in God but one that does not intervene with life except when necessary.

For the first two hundred years of this country, God was the foundation of our society. That is not to say that everything was religious or that our whole society was Christian. Atheists try to claim that is what we are saying. That is not true. God was our foundation because there were certain moral standards that we adhered to that were based on Him. The problem is, that our country was not *completely* founded upon God. If we were, then there would have been no slavery. If we were, there would have been less crime. If we were, there would have been no killing of the Native Americans. If we were, we would have taken care of the poor. These things happened because not all humans claiming to be Christian live exactly the way they should. They fell upon the stone and they fell into pieces.

Anyway, God was our foundation. But around the 1960s things started to change, due to the Baby Boomers. God was being taken out of pieces of our society. God was becoming less and less of our foundation. It was starting to crumble. When God is less of a foundation, it puts a lot of pressure on the family. But the family is not the foundation this world was set on. The family is strong but it starts to lose its power if the foundation it was on is destroyed. And so, look what has happened to the family. There is less love. There is less sharing. And we have seen this. Families now are whatever you can make them. Gangs, extended friends, or whatever makes you feel like you are loved or wanted, will become the family. The nuclear family is hardly around anymore. Families with both a mother and father are now rarities in our society. Marriages aren't even the same anymore. The argument about one man and one woman is almost now in the past. The definitions of family and marriage have now been rewritten. If you disagree and add a Godly view back into the definition you will be seen as a bigot or homophobe. Children used to be considered assets, but now they are considered liabilities.

Figure 10
Family Facts

Family Type	Percentage
Married	48%
Single dad	5%
Single mom	13%
Non-mom/dad	34%

Source: US Census Bureau 2012

As stated back in Chapter 3, the survey I give is very similar to the numbers you see in Figure 10. Those in my survey usually say around 30% are married happily and 25% are still married. That's about 55% being married (compare that to the US Census which says it's about 48%). Barely half of them are coming from a nuclear family. My students tell me about 25% of their parents are divorced. The chart above says 18% are from single-parent families. They tell me that 25% never get married. The chart above says that 34% of people living in the household aren't really even families that are headed by a mom or dad. No matter how we look at this or which chart or survey we get our information from there is one thing that remains constant; the family is being torn apart. The family has nothing to stand on without the right foundation of God.

THE BREAKDOWN

Look at how the breakdown happens. Without God holding the family together what can the family stand on? Love? Love from humans, who only think of themselves? Intellect? The same intellect who says children are basically no better than cancer cells growing until they are delivered? There is nothing that holds the family together better than a Godly foundation. Yes, families can still function but it puts stress upon them. If there is no God in the family then the definition of family is changed because there would be no moral standards that would be similar. The family then starts to turn to the culture for help. But that is the wrong kind of help. The family then starts to lose its importance in society. Once the family starts to lose its importance the culture takes over, gangs become family, laws start to dictate the culture, and the foundation of society starts to really crack.

The culture starts to take control of the foundation and sets up more laws and regulations thinking we can fix the issues with these. They use humanistic duct tape. But we already have seen the issue here. The culture is divided into groups. When groups take over, the division of society becomes even more prevalent. Politics becomes the leading force. They divide us even more. Every issue becomes some political debate and we get nowhere. They bring the media into it and things get escalated. Politicians only say things to get votes, propaganda. They get groups to fight amongst themselves while they reap the support. Groups such as LGBTQ, BLM, and

ANTIFA are used by liberal humanist political activists to gain political advantages. Liberal groups, like labor unions, NOW, Socialists, and Communists, rip into the foundation to take it apart brick by brick. Before people start to tear this page apart, this is not trying to say that those who are homosexual or of any African descent are not important. Black lives matter! Homosexual lives matter! I will repeat. Black lives matter! Homosexual lives matter! But all organizations that have specific agendas that cause some political divisions are the problem. They become political foes and domestic terrorists. Groups start to become violent or threaten the system with separation.

I am forced to hear about Pride Month every year, and I am told that if I don't agree with it then I am a hateful person. But there is no heterosexual parade that is strictly to celebrate heterosexuality, and yes, it would be the same thing. That would be considered wrong though. Listen, if one is wrong then so is the other, especially if it divides us. If you are a homosexual, that is your life. No one should intrude on your life. No laws should ever discriminate against you. That is not a common-sense law and it wouldn't stop anyone from being homosexual anyway. Why create a law that makes homosexuality illegal when all it would do is just make more people criminals? Black lives matter. The organization in its name alone though shows a division. They argued about police brutality, and rightfully so since there have been many discrimination issues. The Black Lives Matter organization seems only to protest when it is a white police officer who killed an African American. All black lives matter. The leader of the group, Hawk Newsome (I'm not judging him for he has a right to be angry), is quoted as saying, "If this country doesn't give us what we want, then we will burn down this system and replace it. All right? And I could be speaking figuratively. I could be speaking literally. It's a matter of interpretation." Watching the riots of 2020, and seeing the destruction of cities was painful to watch, and proves it was literal. People reacted with their emotions (and one can understand why), but they ruled with their emotions. This destruction had nothing to do with black lives matter. The group wants society to change and create new policies and laws. If they can't get it, then those supporting groups like this will tear society apart. I will add more on that later. There is a reason why I said that. And before anyone says that I am biased; I think conservative groups like the TEA party divided us as well. The Neo- Nazis are wrong; dead wrong. Other groups like the KKK are even worse. They have to hide behind the sheets on their head. They back up the worst person in history. And as I stated earlier, political groups are the worst of all because they use these other groups to maintain their control. But why are all of these groups wrong? They are wrong because they have the wrong foundation. They are basing their ideas and emotions on individuals, culture, and the intelligence we are supposed to have.

The breakdown of society starts to cause chaos. Movements that start as peaceful protests become riotous mobs and extremism becomes the norm. There will be more hatred and racism, and no more compromises will happen. Everything starts to become black and white, literally and figuratively speaking in this country.

People think laws will stop things from happening. But no matter how many laws are created, nothing will change unless the hearts of the people can change first. Nothing will change unless the foundation is rebuilt upon the one true foundation. No gun law will work until we change our violent attitudes. No abortion law will work until we change our lustful minds and our views on our promiscuity. No fake news will stop until we stop being so cynical. No real conversations will happen if we hide behind our social media and cell phones. No pain will stop unless we can learn how to show mercy. No love will happen until we learn how not to hate.

Once society has fallen apart the only thing left will be the individual. When society is left up to the individual you have complete chaos. There are no rights and wrongs, everything then becomes subjective due to people having opinions instead of actual morals. We get dystopian societies, the exact opposite of what they thought would happen. Total freedom is not democracy. People think freedom is the ultimate goal, but when this happens and you are not bound by any moral standard then you don't get actual freedom; you get chaos and anarchy.

So, there are those who think they know better, who feel that they can restructure society, one without God. These are the atheist, the humanist, and the liberal. It will not work but in the next chapter, we will see how they have set up or are trying to set up the New World Order, the new foundation.

8
The New Foundation

WITHOUT GOD

I may be wrong, but I often tell people that Hell is not what they think. It is not a place of torment where God is in charge of torturing those who did not listen to Him. It definitely isn't a place where some cool guy in a red outfit with a pitchfork and horns rules over, laughing at all who are there. I tell them I think Hell is a place where God has removed Himself from a person's presence, and the torment that is mentioned in the Bible is because the people there realize that the presence of God is no longer with them. They are in terror because God is no longer with them. The agony (the gnashing of teeth, see Luke 13:28) happens because they know they had the opportunity to be with Him forever, and the chance is gone. Not having God around is something we don't fully know. As long as there is a Christian still alive in this world, we will never know what it is truly like on this earth to be without God. But one day, many will get a glimpse of what Hell is.

2 Thessalonians 2:7, (Amp)

"For the mystery of lawlessness [rebellion against divine authority and the coming reign of lawlessness] is already at work; [but it is restrained] only until he who now restrains it is taken out of the way."

The lawlessness means the world leaving the Law (moral standard) of God. We will become more and more evil as we go. This evil is in the world, but the world does not see it, hence it is being restrained by the Spirit of God. There is a hatred rising against the Christians stemming from the humanists. But once the Holy Spirit (He who is restraining evil) is out of the way, then evil will have its chance. The humanists will take over the structure of our existence. Then the one who is in charge of humanism (the god of this world) will become its leader. But God's spirit is still in the world right now. It is restraining evil. Once the Christians are gone and the Holy Spirit is no longer needed upon the earth, then all evil will be unleashed. That is a world without God; total evil but the world will think it is good.

All the time on the internet forums that I for some reason keep reading, I see atheists always say that they can't wait until the "stone-age mythology" is wiped out and people come to their senses. But even they don't know what it is like to totally live without God. Jesus, though, knew what it was like when He was on the cross. The Spirit left Him. All of the sins were put upon Him and He became our sin. That sin was nailed to the cross and we have been set free. But notice what Jesus cried out during this episode of time.

Matthew 27:46, (Christian Standard Bible)

"Then about that time Jesus shouted, about three in the afternoon Jesus cried out with a loud voice, "Eli, Eli, lama sabachthani?" that is, "My God, my God, why have you abandoned me?"

Jesus felt the presence of God leave Him. He knew the terror of what it was like to not have the presence of God. And if Jesus showed some fear, then Hell is a place I never want to experience. Once God is removed, we will see how horrible this place can and will be.

Man without God means that man takes full control. This can be summed up into one word, humanism. Humanism is a form of atheism. It stresses the power of the human mind and that the human race can live an ethical life without God. "Humanism is a progressive philosophy of life that, without theism or other supernatural beliefs, affirms our ability, and responsibility to lead ethical lives of personal fulfillment that aspire to the greater good." (See resource page) How can one be ethical if there isn't only one standard to live by? It can't be if the definition of being good is left to interpretation. On the atheist website I mentioned earlier, one of the questions that is "answered" by them is "Where does morality come from, if not God?" The group answered it like this, "Morality comes from us - we make it." If that makes sense to you, then go back to Chapter 2, reread it, and then keep reading here. The next sentence from the article says, "The foundation starts with a few biological sources, such as the basic survival instinct, and behaviors of social species." What foundation? How can you have a foundation that starts with nothing, or a cosmic accident?

The biological sources they are referring to are the human race and how it feels. You do have basic survival instincts. That is true. But how did you get that instinct? What exactly is a social species? I guess that means that if you are socially different from someone else, then your morality system will work for you but not for others. Again, do you see the problem there? If we all have different opinions or behaviors then how can there be any solid foundation? How can morals come from us if we all think differently? The site then tries to give an example of how this works. "It's like a family trying to sit down at the dinner table to eat. The reason that it's bad to chew with your mouth open isn't because it was declared in some book, but because it disgusts the other members at the table, to the point that they're less willing to eat dinner with you. Thus, chewing with one's mouth open is deemed "wrong." There is a huge contradiction here. If I deem chewing with my mouth open is ok, then according to their own words, it will not matter what the others think because morality is subjective, right? I would suggest reading the articles on the site, www.atheist-faq.com. It is quite interesting. Not all atheists are humanists but all humanists are atheists.

HUMANISM

Go back to Figure 1 in the Foreword. Humanism can be divided into secular and even spiritual groups. Humanism can actually include "religious" thought and spirituality. Any idea that makes the human race the highest form of existence can be considered humanistic. New Age religions like Scientology and Astrology are spiritually humanistic because they believe in some world or universe order without believing in God. Confucianism is spiritually humanistic because they don't believe in God, but they do believe in Tao, a force that created and leads people to be better. Buddhism is the largest spiritual humanist group there is. They do not actually believe in a god either but have ways for people to better themselves. They have the Eightfold Path that shows how the person can become "Right, Integral, Complete, Perfected" by making vows and promises, understanding your responsibility, and what you can do to help others in life. (buddhanet.net) That website is very interesting as well to tell you the truth. I learned more from that site than I did in all my classes in college on religion.

Humanism though by definition is secular. There are three types of secularism in this world. You have those who live by experience. They want to know all they can by experiencing life for themselves. We call them Empiricists. They do not believe in God because they think that all they experience is due to their own actions. They believe that all knowledge can be gained by us through our senses. You have those who are like Empiricists but only want to experience the best of life such as hedonists and utopians. I call them Utilitarians. It's not necessarily that they just want to experience "with" their senses, but they actually think the senses are the highest form of knowledge there is. Their goal is to feel the most they can. And then there is the most commonly known division of humanism called Liberalism. Liberalism claims to want freedom, understanding, tolerance, and acceptance. They think people should be able to experience life any way they want without interference. Although when you have liberalism in charge of policies you usually get the opposite as history has shown. Liberalism can be divided into those who want emphasis placed on society as a whole called socialism which entails the ideas of Darwinism, Marxism, and Culturalism. We have seen what happens there with places like the Soviet Union and China. And some want emphasis placed on individuality like Egalitarians and Non-Conformists. See my book, *Charting the Three Views of God* for more about these groups.

Humanism emphasizes that life can be lived ethically without God. Humans have the highest intelligence in the known world. We are the highest, well, unless we find aliens from another universe that are smarter. Amazing how they can believe in alien lifeforms but not a Creator. What humanists do not realize is that they have created their own religion. Tell a humanist that and watch them go off on you. Here is what they have done without them knowing about it. They believe humanity is the highest existence. But nature does bind them with the physicality of it all (you know, gravity and stuff). Nature becomes "providence/God-like" since it is in control. They use science/philosophy texts as their "holy" writings. Evolution has become their savior because it is what they feel life is all about and without evolution life means nothing. Intelligence becomes their "Holy Spirit" for it guides them in times of the unknown. To them, people can live morally and ethically without God. What is their foundation then? Below is the foundation that humanism has set up in opposition to the Godly foundation.

The New Chart

Figure 11
The Foundation of Humanism

Individual
Morals, beliefs, personal rights
Society
Cultures, family, group rights
Globalization
Environment, economics, human rights
Mankind
Intelligence

Notice in this structure (Figure 11) the individual is the one in control of morals whereas in the right structure, morals start with God. Those who are humanists do not believe in a one-size-fits-all moral system. That is why it is at the top and not the bottom. This is where the "morality is subjective" concept comes in. How did they come up with this? Well, their foundation is human intelligence. Sorry, I had to laugh there. Human intelligence is the base. That is why you see commercials and slogans like "knowledge is power" or people saying more education is needed to stop bad things from happening. Again, as a teacher, I hope all are educated but just knowing about something will not solve the issues.

Are there good people? Yes. Can someone be a good person without God? Yes. But the question then is, what makes us good? No murder. No lies. No cheating. No stealing. If you don't do these things does that make you good? It sure is a good start. We could come up with a short list that all would perhaps agree on. But after that, we may start to disagree, such as if chewing with your mouth open at the dinner table is acceptable or not. Some believe that marriage is between one man and one woman. Some would say that marriage can be same-sex. Some would say that marriage can be multiple partners. Some say that marriage can be with people less than 18 years of age. Some say that marriage can be anything you want. Which one is correct? How can one be considered good in all of these cases? How can they all be correct? If they are all correct then why would some atheists not agree to allow a marriage of a 40-year-old and a 15-year-old? The answer is that some things are wrong no matter what! Some say abortion is wrong. Some say it is wrong only up to a certain point. Some say it is not wrong at all. Are they all correct? No. They can't be. If morality is subjective then there is nothing that is ever wrong or should be argued about.

If the world allows each individual to make up their own morality system, then nothing can be against the law and therefore all things should be allowed in our culture. Do you know what that is called? Right, it is called anarchy, or dystopia. Have you spotted the pattern yet? Have you seen the issues yet?

Can there be good people? Yes. But do all people fall short of the glory of God and need to have a savior to make them good? Yes. Good may be subjective, but morality is not. I love many people, but I may not agree with their beliefs or actions. The humanist is wrong. There is a morality system. It does not start with the individual; it starts with God.

But now go back and look at some of the things we can all agree with. Is murder wrong? Yes. Lies? Stealing? Yes. Yes. But guess who said it first? It seems like God's law is a pretty good judgment for morality.

THE GOALS OF THE NEW FOUNDATION

Human intelligence as we have studied earlier is limited. If there is no God and all of the bad things we have seen are only caused by human intelligence and not because of man's disobedience, then how does mankind think he will be able to solve all of these issues? The one thing he tries to do is create a system of globalization. If we can pull all of our resources together then maybe we can solve every problem we have. With the intelligence of man that is. Sorry, I had to laugh again.

Globalization is "a term used to describe how trade and technology have made the world into a more connected and interdependent place. Globalization also captures in its scope the

economic and social changes that have come about as a result."
(National Geographic, 2019) We use globalization to try and
bring us together. Economic and social changes are all being
globalized. We can see that in the world today by having world
organizations like the United Nations creating social policies and
the G7 making economic policies. If we put these two words of
social and economic together, we get the main idea of socialism
(sharing human resources to further society but forced sharing).
Socialism is a division of humanism and therefore is atheistic in
nature. In other words, globalization and socialism are forces being
driven by humanism to get rid of God. And we already have seen
what happens when you get rid of the true and right foundation.

The humanist wants liberalism. Liberalism wants individuality,
in theory. But that is the opposite of globalization. The problem
with this structure is that every time you look at another aspect of
it, you can see the contradictions within. If we use globalization
to bring the world together then we are actually setting up a new
world order and that order has to have someone in charge or it
is not an order. How can someone be free with liberalism and
socialism when both are part of the globalization process that will
strip away every one of their freedoms? Are your eyes crossed yet?

Globalization will create this new world order and the only way
to keep control of this order is to divide people further into groups.
Even the fictional world sees this. Look at the series *Divergent*
and *The Hunger Games*. I can't help but watch these movies every
time they are on television and I have read both series. If you don't
know these books, both have a society divided into groups in order
to survive. There is some kind of dictatorial rule that has been set
up due to some failure within society. And oddly enough in both
series, the protagonists realize that division doesn't work. I really

like both the series and the authors. Both of the authors claim to be Christian. In the real world, society is being divided as we live and breathe. We have already discussed the groups and how they divide us. But look at how this new world order/humanistic structure divides us. Society is automatically divided by cultures in this structure. We have so many groups I am surprised we are even still a nation. We have social groups like LGBTQ+, the KKK, and BLM. We have political groups like parties, ANTIFA, NOW, MAGA, and localized radicals and reactionaries that go beyond the liberals and conservatives. We have economic groups like unions, socialists, capitalists, the ACLU, political foundations, and Wall Street. We have philosophical groups. Every time we turn around there is a new group trying to get their voices heard. Worldly speaking, we have alliance systems and economic groups like G7 and OPEC. The world is run by groups seeking globalization.

But the worst part about groups is that at this age and time, the family is not part of our structure. The family has been reduced to a group. The reason why is because the term "family" has been downgraded. We have already looked at the fact that the family is no longer important anymore. It has lost its meaning. It has been torn apart and if you can find a family to belong to then congratulations you found a group for yourself. The family has been reduced to being part of society or even part of the culture when we know that the family should be driving the culture. But there is a new world order that has risen.

A NEW WORLD ORDER

The first major attempt at a global governing body was made on January 10, 1920. The League of Nations was designed to create a way for countries to come and discuss the issues of the world. The main objective was "to promote international cooperation and to achieve international peace and security." The world needed a way to make sure there was a path to some kind of non-violent solution since the last major issue (assassination of the Archduke, Franz Ferdinand) caused World War One. It faced many challenges. The League failed to have the financial capabilities to respond to economic problems. It also failed to maintain any provision to send any military security forces to unstable regions. And on top of it all the newly ascended world power, the United States, didn't belong to the group. In the end, it was a miserable attempt, and had no success whatsoever. The League knew it needed to be dissolved once Hitler could not be stopped. But the idea remained. They needed a new kind of government; one with influence and authority.

Enter the United Nations. When the world has an issue, it is taken to the highest human authority there is. One of the biggest decisions they have made is known as the Universal Declaration of Human Rights. This policy is the driving force of the group.

The examples in Figure 12 are argumentative. They are also

Figure 12
Rights for the New Foundation

Type of rights	Examples
Human Rights	Slavery, Child labor, Genocide, Nationality
Group Rights	Protection from discrimination, Representation
Personal Rights	Voting, Speech, Religion, Protection under the law

Source: United Nations: Universal Declaration of Human Rights, United States: Bill of Rights, personal opinion has modified the categories.

not a complete list. The chart is just to give a small reference to rights being demanded by humanism. Notice the importance and differences of rights. It seems like all we care about is what we can do and who is trying to stop us from doing it. There is no right or wrong about rights as long as we get what we want. If you go to the United Nations website and read "the Declaration of Human Rights" you will see that many of the items, although with good intentions, are repetitive and pushing the limit of enforcement without breaking their own code. I agree with these rights but again, how we do it is erroneous. The Declaration talks about voting, property, religion, and migration across borders. Article 28 of the Declaration says, "Everyone is entitled to a social and international order in which the rights and freedoms set forth in this Declaration can be fully realized." How can you enforce that? Are they going to go to every country and set up a social order? It also says in Article 26 that all education is to be free at the lower level and higher education should be based on merit. Article 24 says, "Everyone has the right to rest and leisure, including reasonable limitations of working hours and periodic holidays with pay." You have the right to rest and leisure. Tell that to the single mom with four children. How are they going to enforce or ensure that? It gets way too involved with each country's ability and autonomy. Human rights are important but I think John Locke had the right idea. We are born with natural rights and they are life, liberty, and property. Everything else is earned.

Group rights are also important but how many groups can we acknowledge that should get equal representation? We have freedom of religion as a personal right but if you belong to a group that feels human sacrifices are needed then how do you stop them in the new world? You have personal rights but when does your freedom of speech become dangerous?

Humanism would say that all rights should be guaranteed. And up to a point, that would be correct. But they would surely strike down the religion that wants to sacrifice people. Don't get me wrong, I would as well but what happened to morality is subjective? The conclusion is that morality is not subjective. There are universal rights and wrongs and those are handed down to us by our true and right foundation; God. Humanism wants to destroy God.

With this kind of structure, we get closer and closer to those dystopian societies we read about. There is no true foundation because if humans are the foundation and we are all different then it is unstable and cannot stand. The only way to get what we need or want is by violence or revolution. THAT IS SOCIALISM.

I teach my students that communism (utopia) is actually a great goal. Imagine if all people were equal and that society was so calm with no crime and no need for government intervention how great it would be. But what they don't know is that that would be Paradise. Paradise is what God intended. Real communism can never be achieved unless God is the foundation and that is exactly the opposite of what Karl Marx said. He stated, "Between capitalist and communist society lies the period of the revolutionary transformation of the one into the other. Corresponding to this is also a political transition period in which the state can be nothing but the revolutionary dictatorship of the proletariat." (Karl Marx, 1875) Socialism is the transitional stage between capitalism and communism he is referring to. Socialism was the stage that would get us to communism, but the only way to do it was through revolution, a violent revolution. We study in class the cases of socialism. We notice that all of them have a few things in common. They all have a dictator. They all have caused death. They all have oppression. They never, I repeat, never get out of the stage of socialism. How then can socialism, a form of humanism, be the answer? It can't. So, what is the solution to the world's problems?

9
The Solution

YOU KNOW WHAT TO DO

My favorite music group of all time is a Christian metal band of the 1980s. The group is called Stryper. They have since regrouped and have become stronger than ever but one of the songs on their first LP/CD was called "You Know What To Do." The song asked a few simple yet important questions. "Are you feeling lonely? Are you feeling blue? Does your life seem empty? You know what to do." We know the answer. We know deep down inside us what is wrong with what we have become. But we are so stubborn and prideful that we don't want to admit anything or change anything.

You know what the answer is. The solution is to turn back to God. None of this is to say that Christians live the right way and are perfect examples of what life is supposed to be. Even Adam and Eve, those who walked with God and knew Him personally still turned their backs on Him. But what I am saying is that we need to reset Him as the foundation of our society. Christians need to go back to the Bible and understand what it means. They need to act more like the Christ they claim to represent and love. They need to rebuild their faith. Faith comes from hearing the word of God but fear comes from hearing the word of man. The word of man is humanism.

We need to reject humanism and not reject the Cornerstone. We need to see humanism for what it really is. It is a satanic ploy to pull people away from the foundation they need to be standing on. Humanism is just a form of atheism. We need to understand that we are not just in a physical struggle with the issues of the world. We are in a spiritual battle for the world's soul. Churches need to be more than just buildings or organizations. They need to become the living organism that God wanted them to be.

We need individuals who take responsibility for their actions. But to do that they have to have the right beliefs. Joseph Prince, Pastor of New Creation Church in Singapore, and one of the greatest speakers I have ever heard, a man who has the insight and knowledge of what God says, has a book titled, *The Power of Right Believing*. He has this saying that "right believing produces right living." If an individual believes in the right things, then his or her mind will transform their actions into the right way of living. Those who do not believe in God are already starting on the wrong foot. They may have the right intentions. They may think that what they are doing is the right thing. And on the surface, they are more than likely not doing anything "wrong." But being humanitarian does not equate with having the right foundation.

We need cultures that are not divided into groups. We need cultures that are driven by the family and ones that do not infringe upon the family. Cultures need to have common- sense laws and not overburden their people with silliness and frivolous laws. Cultures should not separate values, mores, and folkways from the morality of God. The culture needs to be enlightened and not frightened. Political parties need to vanish and people need to run for office based on the values of their community, not their party. Socialism should never be used as a way of life! Capitalism is cruel if left unguarded, but that is where compassion needs to come in and be taught.

We need families to stay together. We need fathers to take responsibility for their leadership and love their spouses and their children. We need mothers who love God, honor their spouses, and love their children. Parents need to teach their children rights from wrongs, both by societal norms and by the morality of God. We need families to build their love on the foundation of God.

We need to remember God is the Creator. God is the foundation we stand upon.

Index

Resources

A Profile of the Baby Boomers in the 90s. (n.d.). https://www.lib.niu.edu/1993/ip930932.html

Alfvèn, H. (2012). *Cosmic Plasma.* Springer Science & Business Media.

Antisocial personality disorder - Symptoms and causes - Mayo Clinic. (2023, February 24). Mayo Clinic. https://www.mayoclinic.org/diseases-conditions/antisocial- personality-disorder/symptoms-causes/syc-20353928

Bondi, H., & Gold, T. (1948). The Steady-State Theory of the Expanding Universe. *Monthly Notices of the Royal Astronomical Society, 108*(3), 252–270. https://doi.org/10.1093/mnras/108.3.252

Can you prove that love exists? (n.d.). https://www.atheist- faq.com/can-you-prove-that-love-exists.html

Cannon, W. B. (1915). *Bodily changes in pain, hunger, fear and rage: An account of recent research into the function of emotional excitement.* https://doi.org/10.1037/10013-000

Chaimweiner. (2014, March 18). *1 – את [Et] – The Most Common Word in the Hebrew Language.* My Hebrew Word הלימ תירבעה. https://myhebrewwords.wordpress.com/2014/03/07/1-%D7%90%D7%AA-et-the-most-common-word-in-the-hebrew- language/

Chan, A. (2013, May 30). Autistic Brain Excels at Recognizing Patterns. *livescience.com.* https://www.livescience.com/35586- autism-brain-activity-regions-perception.html

CHDS School Shooting Safety Compendium. (2023, March 2). CHDS School Shooting Safety Compendium. https://www.chds.us/sssc/

Crow, J. F. (2002). Unequal by Nature: A Geneticist's Perspective on Human Differences. *Daedalus, 131*(1), 81-88. http://www.jstor.org/stable/20027739

Definition of generation. (n.d.). In *www.dictionary.com.* https://www.dictionary.com/browse/generation#:~:text=the%20 average%20 span%20of%20 years,frame%20 periods%20of%2015%E2%80%9320

Definition of Humanism - American Humanist Association. (2019, November 14). American Humanist Association. https://americanhumanist.org/ what-is-humanism/definition-of- humanism/#:~:text=Humanism%20 is%20a%20 progressive%20 philosophy,aspire%20to%20the%20 greater%20 good.&text=Humanism%20is%20a%20 rational%20 philosophy,art%2C%20 and%20motivated%20by%20 compassion.

Diamond, A. (2019, June 24). A Crispy, Salty, American History of Fast Food. *Smithsonian Magazine*. https://www.smithsonianmag.com/history/crispy-salty-american- history-fast-food-180972459/

Divorce: More than a Century of Change, 1900-2018. (n.d.). Bowling Green State University. https://www.bgsu.edu/ncfmr/resources/data/family- profiles/ schweizer-divorce-century-change-1900-2018-fp-20-22.html

Fatbuzz. (2020, November 24). *Human beings need structure and routine - Glen Psychology*. Glen Psychology. https://glenpsychology.com/human-beings-need-structure-and- routine

Globalization. (n.d.). https://education.nationalgeographic.org/resource/ globalization/

Lenin, V. (n.d.). *The State and Revolution — Chapter 5*. https://www.marxists. org/archive/lenin/works/1917/staterev/ch05.ht m

Medicine, I. O., & Research, C.O.O.I.N.D.A. (1996). *Pathways of Addiction: Opportunities in Drug Abuse Research*. National Academies Press.

Morrison, D., M. D. (Ed.). (1995). *The Role of Structure*. https://www. morrisonltd.com/sitemedia/documents/resources/white- papers/role-of-structure.pdf

Mother-Child Bonding Vs. Father-Child Bonding. (2020, April 7). How to Adult. https://howtoadult.com/motherchild-bonding-vs- fatherchild-bonding-15675.html

Penrose, R. (2011). *Cycles of Time: An Extraordinary New View of the Universe*. Random House.

Pew Research Center. (2022, October 26). *America is exceptional in the nature of its political divide | Pew Research Center*. https://www.pewresearch.org/short-reads/2020/11/13/america-is- exceptional-in-the-nature-of-its-political-divide/

Price, M. (2023, June 9). *When did humans settle down? The house mouse may have the answer*. Science | AAAS. https://www.science.org/content/article/when-did-humans-settle- down-house-mouse-may-have-answer

Roos, D. (2023). 'Latchkey Kids': What's Different About Leaving Children Home Alone Now Versus Then. *HowStuffWorks*. https://health.howstuffworks.com/pregnancy-and-parenting/latchkey- kids-children-home-alone-now-then.htm

Scott, E., PhD. (2021). Using Life Structures for Stress Relief. *Verywell Mind*. https://www.verywellmind.com/life-structures-and- stress-relief-3145115

Statista. (2022, August 5). *Entrepreneurial spirit index by generation 2021*. https://www.statista.com/statistics/948469/entrepreneurial- spirit-index-generation/

Susskind, L., & Lindesay, J. (2005). *An Introduction to Black Holes, Information and the String Theory Revolution: The Holographic Universe*. World Scientific.

The Letter Aleph. (n.d.). https://www.hebrew4christians.com/Grammar/Unit_One/Aleph- Bet/Aleph/aleph.html

The New Science of Mother-Baby Bonding – SA Parents Guide. (2022 May 9). https://saparentsguide.co.za/the-new-science-of- mother-baby-bonding/

Washington, G. (1793) *George Washington Papers, Series 2, Letterbooks -1799: Letterbook 24, April 3, 1793 - March 3, 1797. April 3, - March 3, 1797*. [Manuscript/Mixed Material] Retrieved from the Library of Congress, https://www.loc.gov/item/mgw2.024/

WMAP Big Bang Elements Test. (n.d.). https://map.gsfc.nasa.gov/universe/bb_tests_ele.html

9 781944 566470